Exceeds
Expectations

Take Control of Your Performance Review

Tricia Berry & Danielle Forget Shield

EXCEEDS EXPECTATIONS

Copyright ©2010 by 825 Basics™, LLC
orders@newyearpublishing.com
http://www.newyearpublishing.com

ISBN 978-1-935547-10-5 (paperback)
ISBN 978-1-935547-22-8 (hardcover)

Library of Congress Cataloging-in-Publication Data
Berry, Tricia
Forget Shield, Danielle
Exceeds Expectations: Take Control of Your Performance Review
FIRST EDITION

Book cover design and graphics by Rick Marron
Interior design and layout by Val Sherer, Personalized Publishing Services
Edited by Julie Freres Grady

Printed in the USA.

New Year Publishing, LLC
144 Diablo Ranch Court
Danville, CA 94506 USA

Basics™

Contents

Preface vii
Acknowledgements xiii
Introduction. xv

Chapter 1   The Balanced Model 1
Strategies Grid 4
Strategic Communications 5

Chapter 2   Performance Review Preparation 11
Complete the Strategies Grid 12
Complete Your Forms 13
Communicate with Your Manager 15
Have a Plan 15
Take Your Time 17
No Surprises. 18
Request a Follow-up 19
Time to Get Started 20

Chapter 3   Understand the Performance Review Process . . 23
Work Environment 24
Who, What, When, Where, Why and How 26
Manager Dependencies 35
Rating Systems 41

Chapter 4   Explore Workplace Priorities 49
Your Priorities 50
Your Manager's Priorities 52
Your Organization's Priorities 54
Align Priorities 56

Chapter 5   Explore External Performance Review Influences . 67
Your External Networks 68
State of Your Industry 70
Competitors, Vendors and Customers. 70
External Comparisons 72

Chapter 6   Define Performance Review Success. . . . 77
Success for You 78
Success for Your Manager 81
Success for Your Organization 88

Strategy 1   Understand Job Responsibilities **91**

Chapter 7   Define Your Job 93
Strategic Job Responsibilities 97

Strategy 2   Define Goals or Objectives **103**

Chapter 8   Reveal the Real You 105
Likes and Dislikes 107
Strengths 109
Compliments 111
Weaknesses 116
Comments 119
Seeking Feedback 122

Chapter 9   Define Your Goals 127
Dream Job 128
Your Goals 136
Lifetime Goals 138
Five-Year Goals 140
One-Year Goals and Milestones 142
Connect to the Strategies Grid 146

Strategy 3   Collect and Communicate Accomplishments   153

Chapter 10   Collect Your Accomplishments 155
Performance Review Usage – Define Your Needs . . . 156
Accomplishments Reservoir 158
Kind Words and Compliments Bin 161
Curriculum Vitae 163
Resume Update 166

Chapter 11   Communicate Your Accomplishments 169
Identify Your Target Audience 170
Define Your Brand and Promote It 172
Know Yourself 173
Be Genuine in Your Brand 174
Articulate Your Brand 177
Promote Yourself 179
Manage and Nurture Your Relationships 180
Create Visible Value 180
Seek Opportunities to Shine 184
Share and Celebrate Your Accomplishments . . . 186
Connect to the Strategies Grid 189

Strategy 4   Identify and Address Challenges **193**

Chapter 12   Challenges 195
    Opportunities and Threats 196
    Direct Conversations. 197
    360 Degree Feedback. 199
    Personal Board of Directors 202
    Observations 204
    Connect Challenges to the Strategies Grid. . . . 205

Strategy 5   Implement Success Methods **209**

Chapter 13   Complete the Strategies Grid 211
    Summarize the Research 212
    Connect Success Methods to Trends 214
    Connect Success Methods to Job Responsibilities . . . 216
    Your Completed Strategies Grid 219

Chapter 14   Implement Your Strategy 223
    Steps to Successful Action Planning 224
    Begin Your Action Plan 225
    Manageable Steps 232
    Implementation Strategy 234
    Immediate Next Actions 237
    Perpetual Motion Isn't Enough 239

Additional Resources 247
    Table of Action Boxes 247
    Words to Spark Thoughts 249

Preface

Like most people, the performance review process is something I have become more confident about over time. Throughout my career I have enjoyed several managers who really took an interest in the process and in my career development. The worst kind of manager for me is one who seems to cringe at the thought of having to talk to me about my performance. After 15 years in the professional workforce, I thought I had experienced all types of managers. My career has been indicative of the modern workforce and I have changed companies many times. So, I also thought that I had experienced all types of performance review processes.

In addition to my personal experiences, Tricia and I have been making presentations on workplace issues for over 15 years. I have heard the stories of hundreds of people. I certainly believed that I could handle any performance review situation in the most professional and effective manner possible. Then I got another lesson in how important the process we've outlined in this book can be. Especially in how important it is to document your accomplishments and communicate effectively with all those who have an impact on your performance review process.

As Tricia and I were finalizing the first draft of this book, I had just changed companies. I had accepted a position as a Vice President for a start-up division of an international company. From the first interview it seemed that this company did not have a clear reporting structure in place. The U.S. division CEO was fond of a flat structure so that she was aware of and involved in everything. However, she had hired seasoned executives from large corporations who were accustomed to structure. There were obvious expectation conflicts among all of the employees that I should have paid more attention to from day one.

After a few months in my new position, I was surprised when I randomly came across an organizational chart in this flat structure. The bigger surprise was that the chart showed me reporting to someone who was based in another state. I had been recruited by a Senior Vice President in the Houston office who seemed to be directing all of my work activities. I had negotiated the terms of my employment directly with the CEO. I was even led to believe that I was a coworker of the man who was shown as my manager on the organizational chart.

Shortly thereafter, I learned performance reviews were happening. I expected the Senior Vice President I was working directly with or the CEO, both in the Houston office, would perform mine. Instead the person listed as my manager on the organizational chart emailed my review form to me. When I opened the file, I found a four page review form with a total of three review comments. The comments were neither negative nor positive. They simply stated what my job duties were and that I was fulfilling the expectations. The email said that the final form was due to the CEO the following day. I was asked to print, sign and return the form.

I was so surprised by the whole situation and still relatively new to the company that I wasn't sure how to respond. I didn't have the time to contact the people I would normally have asked for advice. I was still trying to determine how my position fit into the organizational chart I'd discovered. The more questions I asked of the various managers, the more confused I became. The conflicting expectations of the formal structure on paper versus the flat structure in play were varied. There was no clear direction.

In the end, I simply printed the performance review form as is and turned it in to the CEO.

Looking back at the situation, I am disappointed that I did not follow my own advice. I should have paid more attention to the conflicting issues in the workplace that were present from the beginning. I could have been more direct in my conversations with the various managers about the organizational chart compared with the reality of my situation. I could have addressed issues as they arose versus being surprised at the last minute. I should have had a conversation with the CEO about my performance review form. Not because it was bad – it wasn't – but because it could have been much better. In the end, I missed the opportunity to enhance my performance review and address the comments that are now part of my personnel file. I was too distracted with determining how and when my manager had shifted without my knowledge. I should have been focused on ensuring my performance was reflected in the review. I should have taken control of my performance review.

Tricia and I both started our careers as engineers and have moved quickly through the ranks of our respective industries. When asked what we do, we both still identify with the engineering profession even though our career paths have strayed from traditional engineering work. Why? Becoming an engineer was a big accomplishment, and one that has given us the confidence to tackle anything that comes our way. It is the foundation for how we address situations and tackle problems. Engineering taught us how to take available information from a variety of sources and creatively solve a problem or generate solutions.

We tend to use this approach in all that we do. From addressing workplace issues and career challenges to managing family schedules, we create processes and seek to increase efficiency. So, when we both hit roadblocks mid-career it seemed logical to do the same thing with the performance review process. The performance review process is all about assembling the information you have, presenting it in a way to showcase your performance excellence, and creating a process that is repeatable and successful year after year.

We've learned along the way that performance reviews differ greatly by organization. They differ even more by the manager performing the review. We have also found that moving up the ladder increases the competition for the *Exceeds Expectations* rating and significantly minimizes the communications received regarding those expectations. I feel confident that my most recent review would have looked very different if it had been written by the Senior Vice President I was doing all my work for rather than the man who hardly knew me or the product of my work. I am also confident that if I had used the process we describe in this book, the results would have been very different and would have more positively reflected my true performance.

After years of encouraging others to use this process, I still need to be reminded to follow my own advice...we all need a reminder. I review the process annually to stay focused on what is important in my workplace and to me. My goal is to take control of my own performance review process. I encourage you to do the same.

Danielle Forget Shield
January 2010

The performance review process is something that I often viewed as a validation of my successes. I have always been driven to work hard and to *Exceed Expectations*. As a young person I often received awards in school and athletics. I was the valedictorian of my high school class. I graduated from college in a down economy and still got the job I wanted. I reached my dream job in my early 30's and have created amazing opportunities for myself along the way. Satisfactory has never been in my vocabulary.

Imagine my surprise and disappointment when I received a less-than-stellar performance review one year. I was in my dream job. I was creating results and I thought I was doing very well. I was shocked when my manager said that he could only rate me as *Satisfactory* in a number of areas because he had no information on my performance.

After reflecting on the past year and the conversation with my manager, I realized that my results were not **visible** to my manager. I had not been effectively communicating my successes. I assumed that compliments about my work would have been conveyed to my manager throughout the year. I needed to find a way to change the situation so that next year's evaluation would reflect my true contributions.

The engineer in me kicked in, and I immediately moved into problem solving mode. I've always looked to create a more efficient and effective process and would use these skills to ensure successful future performance reviews. I developed a monthly communication that would highlight my successes. I learned to document and share my accomplishments as facts rather than intangible comments. I identified challenges early and developed action plans to address potential pitfalls. I created a process that would clearly demonstrate how I was *Exceeding Expectations* throughout the year. My manager would be aware of my successes in every area reflected in the performance review process.

The next year, the process worked and my performance review accurately reflected my successes. All of my performance reviews have since been exceptional reflections of my contribution. It is that process and its success that helped drive us to write this book. Danielle and I wanted to share a strategy you may use in your performance review. It is this process-driven approach that has helped both of us in our careers and will also help you *Exceed Expectations* in yours. I hope you are reading this book **before** you have a negative performance review. I'm confident the process described in this book will help you craft your own strategy for success.

Danielle and I founded 825 Basics™, LLC, to provide superior training and coaching to students and professionals seeking to increase their workplace successes and achieve their career goals. All 825 Basics materials, including the process described in *Exceeds Expectations,* are guided by five principles we believe are critical to success in the workplace and life success:

1. Know Yourself

2. Understand your Environment

3. Strive for Excellence

4. Maintain Balance

5. Have a Plan

Our aim is that all clients of 825 Basics™ gain knowledge and tools that can be immediately applied to their careers and implemented through clearly defined action plans. We will make you think and make you work, but I promise it will pay off in the end. I believe we can all *Exceed Expectations.* It is up to you to make it happen!

Tricia Berry
January 2010

Acknowledgements

We are all a product of our life experiences and the people who have been a part of our journey. The Society of Women Engineers (SWE) has been a constant source of mentors, resources and friends for us and the original inspiration for 825 Basics™ and our first book. We will be eternally grateful for the professional development, inspiration and personal insights we have gained through our involvement with SWE.

Thank you to our families for their continual support and encouragement. Our parents gave us the base of our core beliefs and led us to become successful working mothers who believe we can achieve whatever we want, however we want to do it. Building on this base are our spouses, Chris and James. They provide energy and feedback behind the scenes and play the very active role of working fathers and supportive husbands.

Constantly laughing and maintaining a grounded perspective keep us going when it seems like the only option is to run away. We appreciate our personal board of directors – those fabulous friends and mentors who are always available for a reality check and ready to give honest feedback. Even though they have dispersed around the world, our friends and networks are a constant source of laughter and support with their personal stories. And we are thankful for the time they take to listen to ours.

Many people were invaluable in the process of developing this book. Thank you to all who shared their performance review and other job stories with us. We'd especially like to acknowledge our artist, Rick Marron, our editor Julie Freres Grady and those who provided editing and content reviews: Ann Banks, Irene Chang, Sher Marie Croft, Steve Ginsburgh, Jeff Hobby, Susan Howes, Dr. Kevin Jefferies, Ellen Smyth, and Michele Tesciuba.

Thank you to everyone who knowingly, or unknowingly, became and continues to be a part of our life experiences.

Introduction

"Performance is your reality. Forget everything else."

Harold Geneen, Former CEO
International Telephone and Telegraph

There are so many names for the often dreaded process we all go through in the workplace: performance review, performance evaluation, performance management process, employee development process, performance appraisal, annual review, and the list could go on forever. The simple truth is that rankings, ratings and reviews are a part of our life from the time we are born. In elementary school we are rated on conduct and given a report card. In sports, we are chosen for specially selected teams or end up being the last one picked for playground games. In the workplace, we are compared to our peers and given raises or promotions based on our performance. Regardless of the setting, we all want to *Exceed Expectations* and be acknowledged for our contributions and successes. To make that happen, you must take control of the process and showcase your accomplishments. You must prove you *Exceed Expectations*.

We are going to shift the typical performance review model. In a typical review situation the manager is assumed to have the power. The manager is rating the employee and driving the feedback process. By using the process outlined in this book, we shift the weighted managerial approach to a balance of power and responsibility in the performance review process between your manager and you, the employee. The manager must still be expected to lead and provide feedback, but you can drive the process to your vision of success, so that your goals have a better chance of being met before, during and after the performance review. In addition, you can make the performance review process significantly easier for your manager, an action certain to be recognized and appreciated.

A typical performance review process is often designed to align employee responsibilities and accomplishments with organizational goals. The review assesses your performance and may impact your career development, compensation or opportunities.

I, Danielle, have been in situations where I have been very capable of doing my job, but my attitude had deteriorated my desire to be effective. As a young engineer, I often got bored quickly or did not want to perform the menial tasks required to get the job done. This led to performance review problems because, even though I was capable of performing, I was not engaged in doing my job. As I matured, I realized that I must be perceived as both **capable of** and **interested in** doing my job to succeed at my performance review.

At a minimum, the performance review process includes an annual meeting with your manager. More developed processes may include self assessments, the development of job or career goals, training plans and mid-year checkpoints. By understanding the review process within your organization, you become a part of the process instead of simply having the process happen to you. You can take control because you have the information you need to influence the outcome. Using our Balanced Model, we will walk you through exercises to better understand your organization's performance review process and how you can influence the outcome.

I, Tricia, used the Balanced Model after a disappointing performance review many years ago. I was frustrated because I had amazing accomplishments that year; yet I was marked only *Satisfactory* in several areas since my manager had no information to sufficiently rate me on several of my job responsibilities. Refusing to have this happen again, I began to document my accomplishments, map my work to organizational goals, and communicate regularly and strategically to my manager throughout the year and during the performance review process. The following year I received the *Exceeds Expectations* rating for every job responsibility. I no longer leave the process in the hands of my manager; I take control. Throughout this book, we will describe this successful performance review process and provide the tools for you to do the same.

Just as I, Tricia, experienced frustration in my previous performance review, you may experience a variety of emotions heading into yours. During the performance review, you might be surprised, receiving excellent ratings and constructive career guidance or receiving disappointing ratings and feedback that leaves you confused, angry or hurt. Perhaps you prepared extensively for the meeting, only to be brushed off by your manager who wanted to simply complete the form and mark it off a to-do list. Maybe your manager opened the conversation with your raise and it was more or less than you expected, leaving you unable to focus on anything else during the rest of the meeting. Using our Balanced Model, you should head into your next performance review prepared and confident, not anxious. Because you will be prepared with the tools and strategies in this book, you will minimize surprises and have the information to showcase your performance excellence. Your preparedness should minimize performance review frustrations and put your definition of success at the forefront.

This book offers a process and tools to understand and impact your environment in your specific workplace. This will lead you to *Exceed Expectations* on your next performance review. The process in this book can be used by professionals just beginning their careers and the more seasoned employee who could use a reminder to revisit what they have begun to take for granted.

We all get settled in our ways and need a reminder to take a fresh look at how we communicate our accomplishments to our peers, managers and those outside our workplace. Managers will also find tools they can use with their staff to enhance performance review models in place at their organization and to encourage employee participation in the process. Regardless of who encourages you to *Exceed Expectations* – you, your manager, your peers, or your organization – taking control of your performance review by implementing our Balanced Model will advance your career goals.

To enhance the concepts introduced in this book, the text is full of stories collected from people at all levels of organizations and from all types of industries and work environments. Due to the sensitive nature of performance review stories, we have promised anonymity to the storytellers; but if you see one of our names, Danielle or Tricia, those are our personal experiences. All other stories are real, but we have changed the names or company information to maintain anonymity. We appreciate the candid input from all our participants and encourage you to share your stories with us at www.825basics.com.

Your take-away from this book will be a Performance Review Action Plan tailored specifically to help you *Exceed Expectations* and take control of your performance review. Action Boxes throughout the book contain exercises to capture necessary information from each section. If you need some mental ticklers as you work through the Action Boxes, use the Words to Spark Thoughts at the end of the book to focus your thoughts and get you started. Completing the Action Boxes as you read through the book simplifies the action planning process and will deliver a concise Performance Review Action Plan when you reach the end.

In addition to your Performance Review Action Plan, our aim is for you to better understand the following after working through the book's exercises:

- Who you are, what you do, what is important to you, and what you want in a job

- How your job connects to you, your manager and your organization's motivations, values, priorities, or goals

- How you are perceived and how to market yourself to peers, managers, employees and people outside your organization

- How to communicate all of this effectively and strategically to influence your performance review

- How to repeat the process and continue it throughout the year on your quest to reach higher goals or your dream job

This book is designed for you to work through all of the exercises and put the concepts into practice before your performance review; but if you don't have the time to work through the entire book, skip to Chapter 1: The Balanced Model, Chapter 11: Communicate Your Accomplishments, and Chapter 14: Implement Your Strategy to learn a few quick success strategies. Then start back at the beginning of the book to begin preparing for next year's performance review. This book presents a continuous process that will set you on a path to *Exceed Expectations* and achieve your definition of success.

SUCCESS STRATEGY: Use *Exceeds Expectations* Most Effectively for You

Some people like to use a book as a tool and capture all of their information in one place. Others prefer to use a separate notebook, journal, or specific location where they have more space or freedom to draw, doodle, make notes, and get their thoughts on paper. Consider which style works best for you as you begin working through this book. Whichever direction you choose, keep this book, your notebook, or something you can use to make notes handy so that thoughts can be captured as they occur.

CHAPTER 1

The Balanced Model

"It's not the will to win that matters ...
everyone has that.

It's the will to prepare to win that matters."

Paul "Bear" Bryant,
University of Alabama Former Football Coach

The traditional performance review process is manager driven with the employee and possibly some peers, customers, or clients providing input along the way. Do a quick Internet search and you'll find all kinds of employee review resources for managers and companies: processes, forms, strategies, and even phrases. Little exists to help the employee succeed and take control of what is happening during the performance review process to achieve that *Exceeds Expectations* rating.

Performance reviews are an accumulation of how your manager views the past 365 days of your performance. Your manager must be involved. However, we are going to balance the traditional model and challenge you as the employee to take control of the performance review process. It is up to you to get a high rating on your review; you are ultimately responsible for the outcome. Even though we're challenging you to take control, the best way to be in control is to have regular strategic communications with your manager. Open and honest discussions regarding your performance need to happen throughout the year.

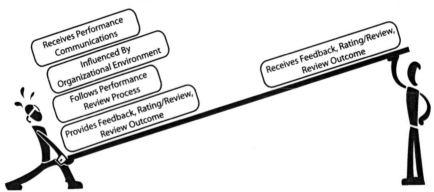

We know work situations vary and there are times when the performance review process may seem to be out of your control. There will also be managers who make the process and strategies we outline difficult or perhaps nearly impossible to implement. However, we challenge you to try. We challenge you to work through the exercises and strategies we describe and you will see a difference. You will feel more in control of the process and your career.

I, Danielle, have been in this situation a few times in my career. I have tried strategy after strategy to communicate effectively with a manager. In the end, I find that even if it seems like I didn't make any progress with my direct manager, I often made a significant impression on another manager, a coworker, or someone who would be an instrumental part of my future. And at the very minimum, I was prepared and confident in my performance review meeting.

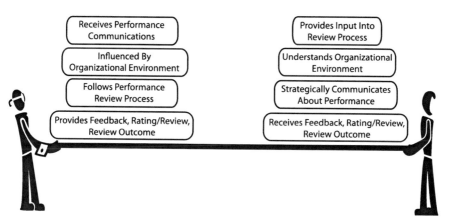

Our Balanced Model centers around five strategies incorporated into the Strategies Grid, a tool for managing your performance review process:

Strategy 1: Understand Job Responsibilities

Strategy 2: Define Goals or Objectives

Strategy 3: Collect and Communicate Accomplishments

Strategy 4: Identify and Address Challenges

Strategy 5: Implement Success Methods

Our Balanced Model is based on you, the employee, being prepared and aiming for no surprises. If you are strategic about your job responsibilities, your performance, diligent in working toward your goals and strategic about your communications, you are in control. You may not be able to rank yourself or provide your own performance rating, but you will know what you have accomplished, where you are headed, and what you need to do to achieve your own definition of success. We are firm believers that we all create our own destinies. Our model provides you with a method to create yours.

Strategies Grid

The Strategies Grid allows you to document your performance review strategies. It is one of the most powerful tools you can leverage to manage your performance review process. It lays the foundation for the Balanced Performance Review Model and provides the connection between manager and employee. It provides details and specific examples that can provide the content and context for your performance review. It provides for structured self-reflection that enables you to better drive the performance review process throughout the year.

The Strategies Grid allows you to capture the important aspects of your job and performance while providing you with a means to track your accomplishments against your goals. It is **not** something that can be thrown together right before your review. Ideally, it will be maintained throughout the year and additions or changes to the grid will be noted as they occur.

The Strategies Grid captures the details of the five strategies of our Balanced Model. As we move through the remaining chapters, we'll go into detail about each strategy. We'll walk you through the model and the Strategies Grid and provide Action Boxes to help you complete the grid. The model begins with your job responsibilities and lays out the goals or objectives, accomplishments, challenges and success methods associated with each job responsibility.

Strategies Grid

Strategy 1	Strategy 2	Strategy 3	Strategy 4	Strategy 5
Job Responsibilities	Goals or Objectives	Accomplishments	Challenges	Success Methods
1.				
2.				
3.				

The Strategies Grid is designed as a strategic communication tool and should be tailored to meet your performance review and career development needs. It is designed as an internal document for collecting the information you need to strategically communicate within your organization. You may want to tailor it to the specific performance review form or process your organization follows. You can add columns such as Skills Required, Status or Progress, or Strengths and Weaknesses. As you use it over time, you may change it, add to it and expand it to meet your needs, but be careful not to expand the grid too much. You want to ensure that you are able to complete the grid and that it is easy to update throughout the year. If the grid becomes too large and too cumbersome, it will not serve its purpose for either you or your manager. The Strategies Grid is your tool – make it work for you.

Strategic Communications

Regular, consistent, strategic communication with your manager is the cornerstone to managing your own performance review. It underlies each of the five strategies of our Balanced Model. How often do you communicate with your manager? You may currently communicate with your manager multiple times a day, once a month or even less frequently. Are these communications strategic? Strategic communications detail progress on your goals and other performance measures at least monthly. You can provide

Strategies Grid Example

Job Responsibilities	Goals or Objectives	Accomplishments	Challenges	Success Methods
1. Manage four projects	Within Budget	Managed three projects within budget	Budget restraints	Expand both scope and budget responsibilities of future projects
2. Sales and marketing of Widget 542	Revenue of $8 million in Widget 542 sales	Mid-year sales of $6 million of Widget 542	Last quarter sales are generally slow	Stay focused on tracking sales and follow up with outstanding order issues
3. Supervise support staff of five	Retain and develop effective employees	100% retention of employees; 90% of employees completed professional development	Project deadlines limit professional development opportunities	Map out professional development opportunities at the beginning of the year and manage project assignments to allow 100% of employees to participate

SUCCESS STRATEGY: Plan Performance Related Communications

Your strategic performance related communications should contain the following information:

- Your first and last name, title or position, location or department, email or other contact information that identifies you if the communication is forwarded to others
- Performance review focused accomplishments such as summarizing the visible value you contributed to the organization
- Performance review focused challenges
- Performance review focused strategies for success that further your accomplishments or address challenges

an updated Strategies Grid to your manager via email. You can also print it and use it in one-on-one conversations. The Strategies Grid is the framework for providing this strategic and updated performance information.

The Strategies Grid provides a means to strategically communicate performance review focused accomplishments, progress updates, and challenges. Accomplishments keep your eye on the *Exceeds Expectations* rating. Progress updates tell your manager where you are and demonstrate how new opportunities may fit into your schedule. Sharing challenges ensures your manager is kept up-to-date on any potential roadblocks that may limit your progress. Ideally, you should list both the challenge and your

Paula is an internal consultant with a large energy company. Her company is very flexible and was tremendously responsive when she requested a home based office rather than relocation across the country. The work situation has worked tremendously well for her personal situation, but she finds it very difficult to stay informed about what is going on in the office. Another disadvantage is that she can have a very successful day and it goes unrecognized. Her coworkers and manager don't see the direct and more immediate results of her efforts.

Paula quickly learned she would need to strategically and regularly reach out to people at all levels of the organization. She developed a weekly email report that she sends to her manager and those currently involved with her projects. The report gives concise and strategic highlights of her accomplishments. Since implementing, she has received several comments about her efforts and successes. Paula learned that consistent communication is essential, especially when you aren't physically visible.

Be strategic and consistent in regularly scheduled communications to maintain visibility.

proposal on how to address the challenge. You want to be viewed as a problem solver and not one who uses excuses. Summarize the value you have provided to the department or organization by visibly aligning your contributions to the departmental or organizational goals.

SUCCESS STRATEGY: Arrange One-on-Ones

We are in an electronic world where emails, instant messaging or other forms of electronic communication rule. However, face-to-face meetings with your manager can provide the best opportunity to strategically communicate your successes. Regularly scheduled one-on-ones with your manager should include discussions about your performance and components of your Strategies Grid. This ensures that you stay connected with your manager's perceptions of your performance. Request a weekly or biweekly 30 minute one-on-one with your manager today.

Strategic communications about your performance often get lost in your day-to-day functional communications. You may communicate about a project daily with your manager, but once a month your communication should be differentiated and stand out from the rest. Use a subject line in your email such as 'May Performance Update – Chris Shield' so your manager knows this is a strategic communication. Take your communication document to your one-on-one meeting so that your manager can use it as a tool for discussion. Send your communication document as a memo through your organization's mail system. Regardless of the format, scheduling or method, be strategic and be consistent.

In some cases, your manager may not thoroughly review the communications you send. You may or may not even get a response. When I, Tricia, created the Strategies Grid and began sending it to my manager, I never received a response. Not even an acknowledgement that the information had been received. I would have loved to have heard back, "WOW! That is amazing information. Thank you for compiling it and sharing it!" The response never came, but I didn't let it deter me. I knew my manager had the information. I also knew it was important for me to have the data compiled and ready for my performance review. I knew I was being strategic regardless of my manager's response to my year-round communications.

Jill is the Director of Customer Service for a large city. As her department has grown, she has promoted from within as much as possible. Jill's team of mid-level managers has become a group of young super stars. While they are all technically exceptional, Jill finds that she is spending more and more time managing and mentoring the group. She quickly recognized that strategic communication is a learned skill that is difficult for most people.

Last quarter, Jill began requiring her team of mid-level managers to turn in weekly progress reports. She rarely even reviews the reports, but has seen a dramatic shift in accountability. Jill knows that the reports will make the performance review process much easier. Her employees might even thank her when they realize that they are supplying her with important information she needs to gauge their success.

Strategic communications detail accomplishments needed for performance review success.

Strategic communications, especially using the Strategies Grid, help you prepare for your review and minimize surprises. They ensure that you and your manager are up-to-date with your

ACTION BOX 1: Write Your Strategic Communications Goal

I will strategically communicate with my manager about my performance _____
(insert timeframe such as weekly, monthly).

responsibilities and accomplishments. Take a minute to complete **Action Box 1** and commit to strategically communicating to your manager.

Chapter 1 Takeaways

The Balanced Model

- The Balanced Model requires you to be prepared and puts you in charge of your performance review.

- The Strategies Grid captures your accomplishments, challenges and success methods for each job responsibility. This demonstrates **visible value**.

- Effective communications are strategic. They have a planned message and planned results.

- Be strategic and consistent in regularly scheduled communications to maintain visibility.

- Regularly communicate with your manager even if you feel it falls on deaf ears.

CHAPTER 2

Performance Review Preparation

"My philosophy is that not only are you responsible for your life, but doing the best at this moment puts you in the best place for the next moment."

Oprah Winfrey, American Media Personality

Although most people don't realize it, participating in a performance review is interviewing for your job over and over, but this time you have the inside information. If we approach the internal performance review process as we did the interview process, we would all excel. Think about the amount of preparation put into interviewing – research on the company, research on the position, research on the manager, defining how you fit into this situation. We often put a tremendous amount of effort into getting the job, but little into maintaining it or truly understanding job tasks as they evolve over time.

Being prepared is essential for success in your performance review. It increases your chances to *Exceed Expectations* and, hopefully, minimizes the stress or frustration often associated with the performance review process. The following four steps will prepare you for the performance review meeting:

1. Complete the Strategies Grid
2. Complete your organization's performance review forms
3. Provide information to your manager in advance
4. Devise a plan for the performance review meeting

Complete the Strategies Grid

In the traditional performance review model, the manager does the bulk of the preparation – completes the forms, prepares the rank or rating, and sets up the meeting. In our Balanced Model, **you** prepare, and **your** preparation is the basis for your manager's assessment. You need to understand the performance review process and how your strategic communications can influence the outcome. You must understand your manager and organization goals and how your responsibilities and performance align. Completing the Strategies Grid will help you be prepared.

Complete Your Forms

In addition to the Strategies Grid, complete the performance review forms used by your organization. Many organizations require employees to complete a self-review form detailing what they have accomplished over the past year. Recognize that a lot of companies have different forms for the self-review and the manager's review. Make sure you have a copy of the form your manager will use to evaluate you. The Strategies Grid may be able to take the place of, supplement or help you complete the self-review form; but you should also assume the role of your manager and complete that performance review form too. This helps ensure you have considered your own performance and the various aspects of the performance review process. Regardless of your work environment and whether separate forms are used or not, completing this preparation step allows you to understand the process. You will be connected to the organizational goals and ensure your communications are strategically aligned to how your performance will be measured, ranked or rated.

SUCCESS STRATEGY: Get Your Review Forms

There are many ways to get your performance review form so you can become familiar with its contents:

- Ask your manager
- Ask a coworker
- Ask the Human Resources department
- Search your organization's website, internal network or other source of organization forms and resources
- Ask your mentor
- Ask a previous manager

Alex had recently joined a new company and didn't know what to expect from his first performance review. In his previous company, the process consisted of a laid back conversation about the direction the company was headed in the next year. So, Alex didn't take anything with him to the review and had only provided the minimum information his manager had requested ahead of time. The review went okay, but there were several places on the performance review where Alex's manager had written, *Does Not Apply*.

Alex was frustrated when he read the review because he felt he had performed in the areas where this was written. However, Alex realized his manager had not been involved in those areas of his work. What his manager had written was completely true. There was no way he could rate Alex, let alone give him the top rating, since the manager had no data to pull from. Alex left determined to not have that happen again. The next year, Alex completed his version of the Strategies Grid, provided it to his manager before his performance review, and took it with him to the meeting in case he needed to have it for any discussion. That year Alex met or *Exceeded Expectations* in all areas of his performance review. There were no places where his manager wrote *Does Not Apply* on the review. His overall rating was the highest possible.

**Be prepared for your performance review
and be strategic in preparing your manager.**

Communicate with Your Manager

After you have completed the Strategies Grid and your organization's performance review forms, inform and prepare your manager. The Strategies Grid, status reports, updated goals or other information related to your performance should be in your manager's hands before your review. Timing depends on your organization and your manager. Some managers complete the forms well in advance of holding review meetings. Other managers may fill out the form in the review meeting. Determine how your manager operates and time your communications so that the data is fresh in your manager's mind when completing your performance review form. If you use the tools and strategies we describe to communicate with your manager throughout the year, this will be an easy step. Preparing your manager in advance will also ensure you have what you need well in advance of your review. You are prepared if your manager needs to change the date or time for your review. More importantly, you are prepared on the day of your review so that you walk into the review relaxed and ready to take charge of your career.

Have a Plan

The final step in the preparation process is to ensure you have what you need for the review meeting to make it successful and less stressful. You should have a two-part plan for your performance review meeting: 1) the process and 2) the outcome. The process determines how you would like the performance review to proceed and what you want to accomplish. The outcome requires you to be prepared with planned reactions or responses. Having a plan will help you be successful in your approach.

You want to go to your performance review prepared with the information, tools and attitude necessary to *Exceed Expectations.* Items you should bring to your performance review may include:

- Paper and pen
- Completed Strategies Grid
- Completed organization performance review forms
- Data, results and references to support your self-review
- Your view of your strengths and weaknesses
- Compliments and kind words
- Career development plan and goals
- Good attitude, desire to grow from the experience, and a smile

Prior to entering the performance review meeting, outline how you would like the meeting to proceed. Make a list of the information you want to share and a list of the results or information you want to receive. While you may not be able to drive the agenda, having a plan of what you want to accomplish can ensure you share or collect information throughout the meeting.

Consider the possible outcomes of the review and be prepared with your responses. How will you respond if your performance review rating is *Exceeds Expectations*? How will you respond if the rating is lower than you want it to be? What if there is incorrect or missing information? By rehearsing these scenarios before the review, before they happen, you will be prepared to respond in a professional and strategic manner. Working through the Action Boxes in this book will help you develop the information you need to be prepared and to create a Performance Review Action Plan.

I, Danielle, have realized over the years that a good attitude is the most important thing I can bring to my performance review. And a good attitude comes with being prepared and confident. As I look back on my various reviews over the years, those that I approached with a carefree attitude were often the ones that did not accurately reflect my contribution and efforts. While those that I was prepared for and entered with a confident smile were the best reflections of the contribution I was making to the organization.

Take Your Time

Once your review is scheduled, block off an hour before and an hour after the scheduled time. Give yourself a cushion of preparation time before and reaction time afterwards. A pressing engagement or project deadline looming will certainly change the pace and tempo of the actual performance review. Allow the time you need to be at your best in the review. If you happen to work for a spontaneous manager who stops by rather than scheduling a performance review meeting, take note of when performance reviews of others within your company begin taking place. Yours is certainly coming soon. Instead of being caught off-guard, prepare early and be ready when the meeting spontaneously occurs.

Once the review begins, listen carefully. Too often we mentally devise our response to what we think someone is saying but we don't actually hear the message. Take notes – it will force you to pay attention to what is being said. Be comfortable with silent times. The review should be a **conversation** between you and your manager to discuss your results from the previous year and your plans and strategy to move forward.

If you need time to read the written review, take the time to do so. Once again, be comfortable with the silence as you read the review and formulate your comments or questions. If you are asked to sign the form or have an opportunity to add comments, be prepared to ask for additional time to read the review and to prepare a response. Practice asking for this ahead of time so it doesn't feel awkward. This is your moment. Be sure to take the time you need to comprehend your review and its implications.

Even if all measurables are marked *Exceeds Expectations*, it is appropriate to read the comments and make any additional notes about successes that might not have been captured by your manager. Remember that this document may one day be used by a future manager to gain perspective about you. Make sure it represents all of your successes. Adding a comment to your review form, if offered the opportunity, is always a good idea. A comment can be as simple as "I appreciate being recognized for my efforts."

No Surprises

Surprises may be fun for a birthday party, but few people enjoy surprises in a performance review. Our Balanced Model and the Strategies Grid aim to minimize and hopefully eliminate surprises during the performance review process. Collecting accomplishments and marketing yourself year-round set the stage for you to *Exceed Expectations* in your performance review.

Establishing communications that solicit feedback throughout the year should prevent you from being blindsided in your review. Providing your manager with strategic information throughout the year **and** in advance of your review should also prevent you from blindsiding your manager.

Even with the best preparation and best communications, surprises do occasionally arise. Surprises may include recognition for a job well done and a promotion you didn't expect. A surprise may also be that your manager asks you about the status of a totally different project than anything you are prepared to discuss. I, Tricia, had a manager ask at the beginning of a performance review, "Where do you see your program in 5 years?" I was prepared to talk about my performance, not about the future of the program I had led for less than a year. I knew enough of the program's strengths and the goals of the overall organization to share a few strategic thoughts. It was enough to satisfy my manager's question and move us back to discussing my performance; however I knew that in the future I would need to be prepared for this type of discussion.

A surprise in a performance review may also relate to some challenge you faced in the workplace. We all make a major mistake or bad decision at some point in our career. Perhaps you selected the wrong vendor for a project and they have royally messed it up. Maybe you insisted that your solution was the only one and it failed. Maybe you had too much to drink at a company event and said something inappropriate. Whatever your mistake, you may need to address it in the performance review process and not be surprised should your manager choose to discuss it. Even if your manager chooses not to bring it up during the review, you should. It is better to acknowledge it and identify what you have done to correct the mistake. Then go one step further and identify what can be done to prevent it from happening in the future by you or someone else. Maybe a process needs to be changed and you have identified a larger corporate issue. Sometimes a problem can be turned into an opportunity to shine. A mistake can be a discovery into how to improve the organization. Don't let this opportunity pass you by.

It is important in the review to take your time, have a plan and request a follow-up with your manager for a later date. You need time to consider comments, and develop a response that is professional and addresses the issues. Your challenge, if surprised in the performance review, is to minimize the surprise and be prepared with a variety of ways to handle the situation.

Request a Follow-up

It is often difficult to digest the amount of information shared in a performance review at the time of the review. Time may be limited and you may not be able to accomplish all your performance review goals during the meeting. You may want to get additional information on some areas of your performance, discuss career development, or share career goals with your manager. While these may be important to you and your career, they may not be

SUCCESS STRATEGY: Dealing with Performance Review Surprises

- Don't react immediately, focus on understanding what is being said and take your time
- Have data available to support your performance results
- Have references who can provide your manager with additional information about your performance
- Be ready to accept the blame if warranted
- Correct the misunderstanding; make sure you understand the situation
- Ask for a follow-up meeting to further discuss the issue or resolution

part of your manager's agenda for the performance review. A follow-up meeting can show you are taking responsibility for your career development and your performance and can accomplish what you may not have been able to do in the review.

Time to Get Started

By moving through the five strategies we outline and describe in detail in this book, completing the Action Boxes along the way and using the Strategies Grid, you will be prepared and surprises will be minimized during your performance review. So, keep your favorite writing tool handy. We will have you highlighting, drawing, making notes and engaging in discussions with others. Chapters 3-6 help you define your workplace environment and personal career aspects. This information will be used as you begin to complete the Strategies Grid in Chapter 7.

Effectively working through these exercises will take time. Some people will find that they need to block time off their calendars, find a quiet place, walk the dog, put the kids to bed, or find a place outside of the office so you can focus on you. You may find that while you are driving, showering, or doodling in a meeting, thoughts and ideas will surface that need to be captured. Keep this book or a notepad with you so that you can record thoughts as they occur. Let's get started!

Performance Review Preparation

- Prepare for your review by completing the Strategies Grid and your organizations internal forms. Consider how your manager will rate or rank you.

- Provide the data you gather early so that your manager can use it effectively in the review process.

- Plan your performance review meeting: plan the conversation, take your time, prepare for surprises, address mistakes made, and request a follow-up after you have had time to reflect on the review outcome.

- Provide comments if given the opportunity. Your review form will remain in your personnel file for future managers to review. Make sure they get the full picture of your accomplishments.

- Be prepared for your performance review and be strategic in preparing your manager.

CHAPTER 3

Understand the Performance Review Process

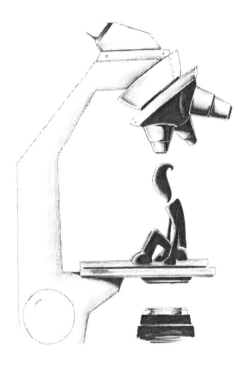

"In the field of observation, chance favors only the prepared mind."

Louis Pasteur,
Greatest Biologist of the 19th Century

Performance review processes span a wide spectrum of rating systems, motivations, and intangible performance factors. They can be influenced by a number of individuals including your manager, your manager's confidants and your peers. How can these people definitively define quality, organization skills, dependability, leadership, communication, decision-making abilities, open-mindedness, effectiveness, energy level, or confidence? The list could span pages, and each organization has its own set of valued performance factors for employees and for specific positions within the organization. How can an employee possibly *Exceed Expectations* when they have no specific measurable gauge? And how can managers effectively judge your skills if they are lacking in any areas themselves or have no way to observe you in all duties of your job? You need to understand how your manager judges each of these criteria. Paying attention to your work environment allows you to align your Strategies Grid to the criteria for which you are judged, and position you to *Exceed Expectations* as you move through the performance review process.

Work Environment

Understanding the internal and external factors that impact your job will help you quantify the intangible performance factors. Your performance review process may be clearly defined. But the differences between your priorities and those of your manager and organization can greatly impact your performance review rating. *Exceeding Expectations* on your next performance review relies on accurately defining your work environment. To define your work environment, you must understand yourself, your manager and your organization better. With this understanding, you will be able to put your performance review and your job responsibilities into context. You will be able to determine how your career aspirations fit within your organization.

Consider your past performance reviews, interviews or other situations where someone evaluated your performance and made a decision about you. Do you have a review or situation that stands out as the best? What about one that stands out as the worst? Use **Action Box 2** to make notes about each of these situations and the attributes or work environments of each situation. Understanding past situations and environments can help you positively impact future performance reviews.

ACTION BOX 2: Assess Past Performance Reviews

List the attributes or work environments of your best and worst performance reviews, interviews or other situations where someone evaluated your performance.

Best Performance Review
Example: I was prepared; My manager complimented me; I received the highest rating

Worst Performance Review
Example: I was not given time to prepare; I did not receive any direction or feedback; I received a low rating

Last Year's Performance Review
Example: Felt my manager didn't understand what I do every day; Received nice bonus; Had good discussion about career options with company

I, Tricia, complete this exercise periodically to reflect upon my situation. In a previous work environment, I found that my best, least stressful performance review situations were those in which I knew what to expect, had clearly defined goals and objectives and had the opportunity to contribute my comments and accomplishments to the process. My worst and most stressful situations were those where I had no information and was unable to contribute to the process. This exercise motivates me to understand the expectations of my manager and have goal oriented and objective conversations with him well before the performance review. Now I better understand the type of environment I must create to have my best shot at *Exceeding Expectations*.

Who, What, When, Where, Why and How

Understanding the who, what, when, where, why and how of your organization's performance review process is important for success. If you do not understand the process used in your work environment, it is hard to understand expectations and nearly impossible to *Exceed Expectations*. You must understand the expectations and what is valued in your organization to excel and advance in your career. How do you do this? Use the questions provided in **Action Box 3** to explore your organization and understand the internal performance review process currently in place.

ACTION BOX 3: Explore Your Performance Review Process

WHO

Who will write your review?	*Example: My manager, Larry Rogers*
Who will present your review to you?	*Example: Member of the review committee and my manager*
Who will read your review?	*Example: HR, future manager, my manager's boss*
Who will have input on your review?	*Example: Customers, peers, administrative staff*
Who are you competing against for rankings?	*Example: Department heads from all areas*
Who are your internal customers? Do they provide feedback?	*Example: Field staff, they provide feedback when something goes wrong*
Who are your external customers? Do they provide feedback?	*Example: Shareholders, feedback provided with stock purchases*
Who is ultimately in charge of your review?	*Example: My manager and ME*

ACTION BOX 3: Explore Your Performance Review Process Continued...

WHAT

What is the rating system for your review process?	*Example: 1-5 with 5 as best*
What is the purpose of the review?	*Example: Bonus and raise distribution*
What is the anticipated outcome of the review – bonus, raise, praise, promotion?	*Example: I'd like a promotion this year*
What is expected of you in this process?	*Example: Complete self-review form*
What data are you collecting to backup your review?	*Example: Feedback from peers and customers*
What does your boss need from you for him or her to be successful?	*Example: Timely information*
What behaviors are valued in your workplace?	*Example: Punctuality, organization, meeting goals*

ACTION BOX 3: Explore Your Performance Review Process Continued...

WHAT Continued

What is different about your current position than your previous position?	*Example: Staff responsibilities*
What is the next step in your career path?	*Example: Project Manager*
What will the review encompass – career development and/or accomplishments?	*Example: Formal meeting to discuss + and – from past year, possibly career options for future*
What are your career development plan expectations?	*Example: Discuss training needs*
What is the path to the top in my company – do I want to be on it?	*Example: I'd like to reach mid-manager level, requires bachelor degree*
What are the metrics used to evaluate employees?	*Example: Educational background, personality*
What was the outcome of your review last year?	*Example: Additional training*

ACTION BOX 3: Explore Your Performance Review Process Continued...

WHEN

When do you receive feedback on your performance?	*Example: In the review meeting*
When during the year will your review happen?	*Example: Fall*
When will your review be scheduled?	*Example: The week before it happens*
When do you need to submit information that will impact the process?	*Example: All year*
When will it be over – how long does the review generally last?	*Example: One hour*
When are questions appropriate in my company's culture?	*Example: In the review meeting*
When are raises determined and given?	*Example: Determined in January, given in March*

ACTION BOX 3: Explore Your Performance Review Process Continued...

WHERE

Where will the review be held?	*Example: Conference room*
Where will you physically be prior to your review?	*Example: In my office*
Where will you physically go afterwards?	*Example: For a break to get a coffee*
Where will the information on your review be distributed – to you, to others?	*Example: HR, future manager, my manager's boss*
Where will the backup documentation for your review come from?	*Example: Our customers and me*
Where are people recognized?	*Example: Annual meeting*
Where will my manager be before my review?	*Example: Weekly staff meeting*

ACTION BOX 3: Explore Your Performance Review Process Continued...

WHY

Why is this process important to you?	*Example: Defines bonus amount*
Why is this process important to your manager, or is it?	*Example: He likes employee development and uses this process to mentor*
Why is this process important to your organization, or is it?	*Example: Rank employees for raise and bonus justification*
Why is the meeting being held – summary of progress meetings or once a year event?	*Example: Once a year corporate requirement*
Why are employees rewarded in my organization?	*Example: Promote loyalty*
Why is there a review process?	*Example: Document reason for raises*
Why do my coworkers like the review process?	*Example: Only time feedback is given*

ACTION BOX 3: Explore Your Performance Review Process Continued...

HOW

How often are performance reviews held formally?	*Example: Once a year*
How often are performance reviews held informally?	*Example: Quarterly meetings with my manager*
How can you maximize the outcome of the process?	*Example: Provide accomplishments ahead of time*
How can you communicate effectively with your manager?	*Example: Email reports*
How can you alter an incorrect perception that has developed?	*Example: Understand the situation better*
How has your position changed in the past year?	*Example: Doubled number of accounts*
How are yearly goals handled in your organization?	*Example: Distributed by my manager*

ACTION BOX 3: Explore Your Performance Review Process Continued...

HOW Continued...

How are yearly goals judged by your manager?	*Example: Don't seem to be that important*
How are competencies handled?	*Example: Each job description has a list of required competencies*
How does your manager view the process?	*Example: Manager seems to enjoy performance review process and providing feedback, especially negative feedback*
How can I make the review process easy for my manager?	*Example: Provide my completed form with backup data*
How are questions asked appropriately in my organization's culture?	*Example: Direct and clear questions get the best result*
How do I highlight my accomplishments without threatening others?	*Example: Present facts*
How can I integrate feedback I've received throughout the year in this process?	*Example: Note how I have integrated previous feedback into comments section of review form*

You may not be able to answer all the questions in Action Box 3 yet, but you will as you continue through this book. The ways in which you can influence the performance review process and its outcome will become more apparent as you complete the strategies and Action Boxes.

Manager Dependencies

The internal performance review process at your workplace can be dependent upon your manager. Some managers will provide feedback continually without a formal process. Others cringe at the thought of confronting an employee or providing suggestions to improve performance. Within a single organization you will find managers that run the full spectrum and as your position changes within the organization, you will need to adjust your expectations and adjust to the performance review style of your manager.

I, Danielle, have experienced this multiple times. One particular experience was a transition from a manager who was actively involved in my activities to one who had no interaction with me. With the first manager, I saw him weekly and we talked several times a day. He had the same interaction with all his employees and his managerial style was to provide lots of feedback. I was promoted and my new manager had no interaction with me. We saw each other very little and may have spoken on the phone once a month. As you might gather, I received minimal feedback from him. It became my responsibility to increase my strategic communications to keep my new manager informed.

If this is the first time you will be reviewed by your manager, do as much research as possible. Talk with others who have gone through the review process with him or her. Each manager may have a different style or approach, even within an organization where the process is clearly defined. The better you understand the system and your manager before the review, the better prepared

When Julie graduated from college, she was recruited to work in a rotation program with a high-profile oil company. Her first manager was very hands-on and gave continual feedback to improve both her technical and soft skills. Julie was diligent about incorporating this feedback into her daily work. When her first performance review occurred, there were no surprises. It was simply a review of the previous year and goal-setting for her future.

As Julie was promoted through the organization, she encountered managers who were not as open with feedback. Some even seemed to cringe at the idea of providing comments when asked, but she continued to receive high ratings on performance reviews. The higher Julie moved in the organization, the less feedback she received and the more difficult it became to gauge how she was performing on a daily basis. Julie became frustrated with the system and quit making an effort to solicit feedback which, in turn, minimized how she communicated her successes. After 10 years of excellent reviews, she received a very negative review with very little feedback – simply checkmarks in places she had never seen them before. Julie was speechless. In her opinion, she was still performing at the same exceptional rate she always had, but what she didn't recognize was that her environment had shifted. After taking some time to recover emotionally, she stepped back from the situation and evaluated her options.

Julie recognized that she had a bright future if she could find other ways to solicit and receive feedback that were more in line with her new responsibility level. Julie learned to pay more attention to the office chit-chat and activities going on around her. She recognized who was selected to participate in certain activities and why they were selected. She began to see what was valued by the new set of managers. Julie now understands that as her environment changes, she must make shifts to maintain visibility and recognition.

Your environment is dynamic, not static, and your performance review strategy must adjust accordingly.

you can be – you improve your chances to *Exceed Expectations* on your review.

To have to research your manager's methods may seem like a daunting task, but it may be fairly easy if you've developed relationships with your coworkers. You could ask the person who seems to be the most successful in your group to have lunch and discuss the process and your manager's style. You could ask another new person to the group if they have heard anything about your manager's style. If you are not new to the company, but just to the manager, ask your previous manager for advice or tips on working with the new one. And you can always run Internet searches on your manager's name and try to find a bio. You can learn a lot about a new manager from his or her volunteer activities, the charities he or she participates in, or the conferences where he or she makes presentations. You simply need to do your homework before entering a performance review with a new manager. Use **Action Box 4** to record the information you find or know about your manager's performance review style.

ACTION BOX 4: Identify Your Manager's Performance Review Style

What is your manager's performance review style? Refer to Action Box 3 for the who, what, when, where, why and how questions, if needed.

Example: Fair; Open; Honest; Evasive; Predictable; Harsh

Elizabeth is a public relations manager. She recently left her position at a large firm to join a fairly new start-up company. This was an exciting opportunity to work with a group of people she knew from previous positions, but had never worked with directly. At the large firm, performance reviews were taken very seriously and a formal process was in place that included employee input and career planning. After four months in her new position, Elizabeth was walking out of her office to go meet a friend for lunch when her manager stopped her and asked if she had a minute. Still new to the position and wanting to make a good impression, she returned to her office for a quick talk with her manager. As they sat down, Elizabeth's manager handed her a completed performance review form and asked her to sign it so he could get it turned in to Human Resources.

Elizabeth took the form and was horrified by what she saw. *Needs Improvement* was marked in several locations that she had always excelled in under previous managers. She explained to her manager that she was late for an appointment, but would like to have a conversation about what he thought she needed to do to improve her performance. Elizabeth's manager made it very clear that he would not be altering the ratings or explaining them. If she disagreed, she was free to make notes in the comments section of the form. Elizabeth completed the comments section later that day and returned it to her manager.

After taking a few weeks to calm down, Elizabeth stepped back and began to observe the office dynamics. The people Elizabeth worked directly with were not the confidants of her manager. The people her manager relied on for information only knew her from brief encounters, some of which had not been on the best of terms. Elizabeth recognized that if she wanted to excel in this environment, she would need to learn how the system worked in her new company. She would also need to develop her own system to effectively communicate successes to her manager and have those successes affirmed by the people he relied on for advice.

Understand your manager's performance review style and advisors so you can align your communications and influence the review process.

Determine who advises your manager on your performance. Many managers will seek input from your peers, other managers, and your staff or associates before finalizing your performance review. Find out in whom your manager confides, respects, listens to, and relies on for feedback and information. You must ensure these people are providing the right feedback on your performance. It is also your responsibility to make sure those who do not directly influence your manager can offer positive unsolicited feedback on your performance.

Ryan works as a project manager for a large engineering firm. Although no employees report directly to him on the organizational chart, he manages the technical activities and accomplishments of a lot of his coworkers throughout the year. As each project is ending, Ryan solicits written feedback from members of his team. Ryan's main objective is to collect information to continually improve future teams and his own performance.

Recently Ryan received an unexpected *Needs Improvement* on organizational skills on his performance review. He was especially taken by surprise because this was one area where his team members had often given him very high ratings and made verbal comments about his skills. Because he had collected the information from his previous team members and kept it, he was able to share this data with his manager. Ryan presented the data and asked his manager what the rating was based upon. It turned out that one of the confidants of Ryan's manager had asked Ryan for a document one day and he didn't provide it as quickly as the person expected. This unmemorable event for Ryan was interpreted and communicated as a lack of organization skills. Being able to provide written feedback from people who had worked directly with Ryan allowed him to change the perception of his manager and the rating on his written review form.

Document your accomplishments and share them with your manager before your performance review.

Use **Action Box 5** to list your manager's confidants and your relationship with each of them. In the later Strategies Grid exercise of collecting and communicating accomplishments and implementing success methods, we'll refer back to these influencers, but you must first understand **who** they are and **how** you may connect with them through the relationships and networks you have in place.

I, Danielle, encountered a difficult situation with my manager's confidants early in my career. My manager's husband worked with my father. When my father was at his work functions that included spouses, I would often come up in conversation. Simple comments by my father, such as "Danielle gets bored easily. Make sure you challenge her." were often misinterpreted to mean that I was complaining to my father about being bored at work. Managing that relationship became the most difficult part of my job.

If you are not sure who may influence your manager, observe who he or she goes to lunch with or meets with frequently. Who does your manager defer to when making decisions or seek out for mentoring and advice? Pay attention to who your manager sits next to in meetings or engages in casual conversations with. Understanding your manager's influencers can provide insight into what your manager values, the style of work your manager appreciates or the way your manager communicates or likes to receive communication. This understanding can aid you in strategic communications about your work and your performance.

The performance review process is influenced by a wide variety of people. By understanding your manager's influencers, you understand who is taking part in your performance review.

ACTION BOX 5: Describe Your Manager's Influencers

Who are your manager's confidants? Describe your relationship with these people and how you can include them in your strategic communications.

Manager's Influencers	Your Relationship/Communications With Influencers
Example: Mary Delaney	Example: Only met her in passing, but know her assistant very well

Rating Systems

The performance review process and the rating you receive can determine your ranking within your overall organization. Your rating may impact your salary, raise or bonus. It may also impact future promotions, job opportunities and compensation. Each workplace uses the data collected in a performance review process differently. For some companies, it provides a talent inventory to pull from for promotion opportunities. Some workplaces have "up-or-out" systems where the top percentage is promoted and the bottom percentage is terminated. Some larger organizations have a forced ranking system. Managers are required to meet, discuss each other's employees and essentially fight for ranking status for each employee. The rank or status of each employee may never be intended to serve as a marker by your manager, but a situation may arise where the intention changes. When layoffs become imminent or your management changes, a performance review may be the only voice of the employee.

Performance review ranking systems may rank employees solely against their own goals and expectations or rank all employees in some sort of top performer to bottom performer order. The ranking system may include some components of each of these methods. I, Tricia, have experienced a version of both systems in my career. At a previous employer, all employees were ordered by percentages with the top performers receiving scores above 90%. Rankings were based on performance against defined personal and organizational goals and metrics. A higher score equaled a bigger raise. At my current employer, each employee is rated individually on a scale ranging from *Does Not Meet Expectations* to *Good Solid Performance* to *Exceeds Expectations*. Rankings are more subjective with no defined goals or metrics other than those I infuse into the process. A higher score has no current impact on compensation as merit raises have been eliminated in recent years. In the previous job, I was easily motivated to *Exceed Expectations* because the ranking system rewarded me for my efforts. In my current job, I must choose to be more self-motivated because regardless of the ranking system used, we are all replaceable.

While my current job does not tie ranking to compensation, I could easily be replaced should I receive the *Does Not Meet Expectations* ranking repeatedly. If my peers *Exceed Expectations* by publishing papers, my manager may rank my performance lower if I do not do the same. Understanding your environment includes understanding the skills and abilities of those around you and understanding how others *Exceed Expectations*. This understanding can influence how you craft your strategic job description and position yourself at the top of the pool as a critical contributor to your organization. When a manager is rating his or her employees, the system ultimately requires a comparison and ranking of others at the same level or in the same type of role. Learn from those around you to determine how you can shine. Communicate how you provide value so that you can *Exceed Expectations* in your review.

Zane wanted to be an attorney for as long as he could remember. His dream was to become a Partner in a major law firm. Zane worked long hard hours as a young associate and participated in every activity he was offered. He believed that all his hard work would pay off when he reached the Partner level and had a group of associates to do all his work for him. Shortly after Zane was named a Partner in the firm, he started to realize that things were only getting harder and more political. Now he not only had to fend for himself, but also for the associates who reported to him. That first year as a Partner opened his eyes to a lot of the office politics he had missed when he was working so hard to reach his own goal.

Nearing his first anniversary as a Partner, Zane participated in the annual meeting to determine which associates would be elevated to Partner the next year. He quickly realized that the attorneys who worked the hardest or were the smartest were not necessarily the ones being selected for promotion. Instead it was the people who had developed other skills, such as networking, bringing in new clients, growing work from existing clients, and becoming someone that everyone enjoyed being around. Zane was grateful that someone had helped him develop these skills, although he thought they were a waste of time prior to this meeting. Now he realized that he was being ranked based on skills he hadn't realized were so important.

Understand what skills are valued in your workplace and how you compare to your peers.

Consider the valued skills of your peers and how they *Exceed Expectations* or get recognized for the work they do. Make note of these skills in **Action Box 6**.

Rankings often impact compensation. Regardless of the size of your organization, there is often a budgeted overall raise and/or bonus pool for all employees in the company. For example, your

SUCCESS STRATEGY: Determine Your Coworker's Valued Skills

There are bold and subtle ways to determine what is valued about your coworkers:

- Ask your manager

- Ask a coworker

- Observe situations in which people are complimented

- Consider what you value in each coworker

- Pay attention to office gossip – people's strengths and weaknesses are often highlighted in general chit-chat

- Trust your intuition – what values do you notice people have

ACTION BOX 6: Identify Valued Peer Skills

What are the valued skills of your peers? How do they *Exceed Expectations* or get recognized for the work they do?

Example: Don't rock the boat; Socialize with peers outside of work; Open and honest with feedback; Expert in web development software; On cutting edge of new technology

Raise Calculation Example

Employee	Current Salary	Raise Percentage	Raise Amount	$ Over/ Under %
You	$100,000	6%	$6,000	+$3,000
Coworker 1	$100,000	3%	$3,000	$0
Coworker 2	$100,000	2%	$2,000	-$1,000
Coworker 3	$100,000	2%	$2,000	-$1,000
Coworker 4	$100,000	2%	$2,000	-$1,000
Total	$500,000		$15,000	$0

company may budget an overall 3% raise for all employees. If the total payroll in your company is $500,000, then the total raise pool that can be allocated to all employees is $15,000. If your manager wants to give you a 6% raise, he must give other employees raises lower than 3%.

These formulas apply to raise and bonus calculations. Once you understand these calculations, it becomes apparent that you must constantly outshine your coworkers. In a large corporation, you may need to outrank both your direct peers and the hundreds or thousands of employees across the organization.

Determine the rating structure within your organization. Does the rating range from *Below Expectations* to *Exceeds Expectations*? Is it based on ranking employees within performance percentiles (top 5% performers, bottom 5% performers)? Is your salary, bonus, promotion or other benefit based on your performance review rating? Examine your organization's performance review form or visit with your manager to better understand the rating process. Use **Action Box 7** to describe your organization's rating structure.

The performance review is the most powerful tool your manager has to fight for you to be at the top of your organization's rating system. Because of this, your performance review should

ACTION BOX 7: Describe Your Organization's Rating Structure

Rating System	Reward Mechanisms
Example: Below Expectations to Exceeds Expectations; Bottom 5% performer to top 5% performer	*Example: Salary; Bonus; Raise; Promotion*

As a young engineer, Gary received a 10% raise during a recession. Although this was considered to be an excellent accomplishment, Gary was unhappy with the dollar amount of the raise. He met with his supervisor to express his dissatisfaction. His supervisor was incredulous that Gary was unhappy with the amount and shared that he (the manager) had only received a 2% raise. Later Gary did the math and realized that his manager's 2% raise was still a greater dollar amount than Gary's 10%.

Gary was unfamiliar with the concept of the raise pool and the formula used within his organization. Gary could have used the meeting with his supervisor to better understand the raise formula used by his company. He could have asked how to improve his performance or advance his career through other reward mechanisms, such as a promotion or additional vacation time. He also could have asked for a follow-up meeting after doing the math. Instead, he took the supervisor's 2% raise explanation and his later realization of the dollar implication and stewed over it. Feeling unappreciated, Gary eventually left the company for a fresh start elsewhere.

Know the rating system within your organization. Seek to understand your performance related compensation or other reward mechanisms.

be something you take very seriously. It is up to you to understand the rating system in your organization and the work environment in which you will be evaluated. Completing the Strategies Grid and Action Boxes in this book will help you move to the top.

Chapter 3 Takeaways

Understand the Performance Review Process

- Knowing what metrics you will be gauged on allows you to convey the appropriate accomplishments to your manager.

- Document your accomplishments and share them with your manager **before** your performance review.

- Defining the internal and external factors that impact your job demonstrate your understanding of your environment. Know the who, what, when, where, why and how of your workplace.

- Understand your manager's performance review style and advisors so you can align your communications and influence the review process.

- Know the rating system within your organization. Seek to understand your performance related compensation or other reward mechanisms.

- Your environment is dynamic, not static, and your performance review strategy must adjust accordingly.

CHAPTER 4

Explore Workplace Priorities

"I will not allow yesterday's success to lull me into today's complacency, for this is the great foundation of failure."

Og Mandino, "Sales Guru" and Best-Selling Author

In the performance review process, it is important to understand what is valued by all those with whom you interact. Especially important are the priorities of your manager and your organization. And let's not forget about you. What do you value in the workplace? Understanding your own priorities and those of your manager and organization allows you to effectively communicate about your performance and direct your career along the path you desire.

Your Priorities

Understanding how others perceive you is critical. To use this information to your advantage in the performance review process, you must also understand what you value in your current work situation. Your priorities can drive how you proceed through the performance review process. They can help prioritize the actions you need to take to *Exceed Expectations* in all areas of your job or just those areas of greatest importance to you.

I, Tricia, am perfectly content in my current work situation. I have children in school and have the flexibility within my job to take-off when I need to pick them up or attend a school function. I value the flexibility I have and the freedom to get my job accomplished in a way that works best for me. In the past, I would have been motivated by pay increases, job titles and recognitions. My motivation now is to do a fantastic job in my current position and to exceed my own expectations in the work that I do.

What motivates you to get up and go to work every morning? What priorities do you value in your work environment? The potential list of factors is endless and the set of factors are unique for each individual. In **Action Box 8**, list your top 10 workplace motivators. Some common items people list as top priorities in the workplace include:

- A paycheck
- A challenge
- Somewhere to go
- Something to do
- Friends at work
- Work is fun
- Work is exciting
- Medical benefits
- Love the industry
- Gaining new skills
- Future opportunities
- Recognition
- Achievement
- Feeling important
- Making a difference

- Making a contribution
- Advancement
- Security
- Winning
- Competition
- Teamwork
- Creativity
- Being well-known
- Freedom
- Mental peace
- Helping others
- Integrity
- Belonging
- New car

- Personal development
- Personal fulfillment
- Professional fulfillment
- Professional network
- Power
- Personal identity
- New furniture
- Learning
- Status
- Title
- Job perks
- Feeling empowered
- Being the boss
- Fulfilling a goal

ACTION BOX 8: Recognize Your Workplace Priorities

List your 10 most important workplace motivators or priorities.
Examples are provided above.

1. _____
2. _____
3. _____
4. _____
5. _____
6. _____
7. _____
8. _____
9. _____
10. _____

Brian's career in finance had progressed quickly. He was well known as a hard worker and someone who could be counted on to always get the job done. He accepted advancement opportunities and location moves throughout his career to gain experiences. He was motivated by the experiences rather than the salary increases associated with many of his moves. Everyone around him knew he was on the fast track to become the CFO of the company.

As he was moving up the ladder and frequently moving to new locations, Brian met and married Katrina. After four years of marriage, Brian and Katrina were very excited about the birth of their first child. As their family and Brian's career continued to grow, the moves became harder on everyone. A stable position and salary became more important than advancement, bonus or stock potential. Brian never thought he'd reach a point in his career where he'd be content to stay in a position that wasn't his ideal job or the right number of zeros on his paycheck. But here he was. The most surprising thing to Brian was that he was okay with it because he loved spending time with his family. Brian also realized that his personal life would settle down eventually and his top workplace priorities would likely shift again. But for now, understanding his motivation of staying close to family with a stable and great paying position allowed him to satisfy his personal needs and adjust his career expectations.

Motivations and priorities may shift over your career.

Your Manager's Priorities

Once you have identified your workplace priorities, compare them to what your manager appears to reward in the workplace. What does your manager value in his or her job, employees or boss? What motivates your manager to go to work every day? Your manager may have many of the same priorities you do. Perhaps your manager values a successful organization and stellar employees so he or she can continue to advance. If you understand your manager's priorities and workplace drivers you will understand how to communicate with your manager and to *Exceed Expectations* on your performance review.

Some people are very familiar with their manager and will find this exercise to be easy. Others will struggle with determining what is important to their manager. Whether you are confident in your assessment or not, you should verify this information before you depend upon it for your performance review. The easiest thing to do is to ask your manager. Possible questions are:

- What do you value in your team members?

- What type of communication would be most effective?

- What can we expect from this reorganization?

- How does our department fit into the organizational structure?

You can also learn a lot about your manager by paying attention to what is happening around you in the workplace. A manager who schedules workplace meetings and events around family activities may prioritize balance. A manager who arrives early and works late may consider hard work or dedication a top priority. Observe your manager's actions and communications to deepen your understanding. Pay attention to how your manager facilitates meetings and follows meeting agendas. What is discussed or ignored? Notice the metrics your manager tracks and how your manager rewards people in your department or team. Which accomplishments get recognized, what projects get attention? Take note of office chit-chat involving your manager and the topics of office gossip.

I, Danielle, had a hard time understanding what motivated a previous manager. Due to the nature of my job, I rarely saw my manager and only spoke with him once a week. By getting to know my coworkers and paying attention to their comments, I gained better insight on what my manager valued. I developed relationships with people who interacted with him much more frequently than I did. I used those relationships to gauge anticipated reactions to situations and how my progress was being measured. I learned a lot by simply paying attention to what was happening around me.

Use **Action Box 9** to list your manager's most important workplace motivators. Repeat this exercise regularly because family situations, lifestyle, unseen job pressures and drive to succeed can quickly alter priorities. Once you better understand the driving force behind your manager's actions, you can adjust your communications, adjust your performance or, in some cases, assist your manager in such a way that you easily show how you *Exceed Expectations*.

Your Organization's Priorities

Why does your organization exist? Your organization may have stated goals and objectives. Your performance review may be tied to various organizational metrics driven by your organization's goals and priorities. Explore the priorities of your organization by exploring, not only what is publically stated, but also what you observe. Consider the following methods to gain insight into what your organization values:

- Thoroughly review your organization's website, annual report or shareholder reports
- Conduct Internet searches on your organization and senior management to discover what others are saying about them
- Read industry articles about your company
- Review the marketing materials distributed by your organization

ACTION BOX 9: Note Your Manager's Priorities

List your manager's 10 most important workplace motivators or priorities.

Examples are provided on page 51.

1. _____

2. _____

3. _____

4. _____

5. _____

6. _____

7. _____

8. _____

9. _____

10. _____

- Pay attention to casual office chit-chat

- Pay attention to industry gossip at conferences and meetings

- Review recruiting materials or what is told to potential candidates

- Discover what your organization rewards by evaluating internal metrics used: sales, earnings, safety, production, customer satisfaction

Organizational priorities often use a different language than personal priorities:

- Generating revenue

- Generating profits

- Being an industry leader

- Accomplishing a specific goal

- Pleasing customers

- Doing the right thing

- Achieving high performance ratings

- Reaching a specific financial metric

- Keeping investors happy

- Keeping employees happy

Use **Action Box 10** to list the results of your research. What are the top motivators or priorities of your organization?

I, Danielle, found this exercise to be very difficult as a young engineer. I worked for a very large consulting organization floating between three different departments. Each department seemed to have a different set of priorities and rules. Identifying the overall corporate strategy required that I step back from my micro view and see the big picture. Satisfying customers, providing an exceptional work product and being known as a technical leader seemed to be at the core of everything that was rewarded. This information changed the way I approached my job.

Align Priorities

After exploring your motivations and priorities and those of your manager and organization, compare them to discover alignment or disconnects. Do your priorities align with your organization and manager? Can you operate within your organization and your current situation in order to *Exceed Expectations*? Use **Action Box 11** to make this comparison.

Now that you have defined the alignment or lack of alignment of priorities between you, your manager and your organization,

ACTION BOX 10: Describe Your Organization's Priorities

List your organization's 10 most important workplace motivators or priorities.

Examples are provided on pages 55 & 56.

1. _____

2. _____

3. _____

4. _____

5. _____

6. _____

7. _____

8. _____

9. _____

10. _____

consider which of the following categories apply to you for further understanding.

Category 1: Your Priorities and Your Organization's or Manager's Priorities Are the Same

Congratulations! This is a nice position to be in. Highlight these alignments and how you contribute value with your accomplishments when sharing your performance updates with your manager. For example, if a priority you share is to be an industry leader, then be sure to communicate how you are leading within the industry and contributing to your organization's being an industry leader. Show how you are generating patents, contributing to technology, advancing the research, or leading in service.

ACTION BOX 11: Compare Priorities

List the priorities you identified in Action Boxes 8, 9 & 10 and identify the common priorities.

Example: Hard work is valued by my manager, my organization, and me.

	My Priorities	My Manager's Priorities	My Organization's Priorities	Common Priorities
1				
2				
3				
4				
5				
6				
7				
8				
9				
10				

When priorities are in sync, it is easy to become complacent. There are many personal and professional changes in life that can alter what people highly prioritize – and there are many industry, financial or other changes that can alter what your organization considers a top priority. Keep your eyes and ears open for changes. Repeat Action Box 11 quarterly to help you maintain this comfortable position. Ensure your communications about your performance are in alignment with your manager and your organization.

Robin is a senior manager with a telecommunications company. Early in Robin's career she joined the Research & Development (R&D) division. Her primary motivation was to move up within the organization by proving her technical capabilities. She worked very hard to prove herself and was focused on the success of her company and its products. Robin made special efforts to ensure that her manager and company were highlighted as sharing in her successes. Her efforts continually paid off as she was promoted and recognized with awards both within and outside her company.

Once Robin felt she had achieved her goals within R&D, she decided to expand her skills by pursuing a Masters of Business Administration. She was surprised when she thoroughly enjoyed the business classes. Every class she took changed her perspective on how she had been taught to achieve success at work and what success really meant to her. The class experience also altered her career path ambitions. Robin began looking for opportunities inside and outside of her company that would allow her to apply her new skills.

By recognizing how her workplace priorities had changed over time and how her new career path ambitions differed from her current track, Robin was able to successfully shift gears. She communicated her new career goals to her manager. Robin's manager helped her move into a position that was more closely aligned with her new priorities, but also used the skills she had proven in her previous positions. Robin continues to *Exceed Expectations* because she communicates how her priorities are aligned with management and her organization.

**Pay attention to your current work priorities
and share changes with your manager.**

Category 2: Your Manager's Priorities Are Not the Same as Yours

In this situation, find common ground. What priorities do you have in common? Even if they aren't the top priorities on the list for either you or your manager, finding common ground can give you a starting place for conversations and a lens through which to share your experiences and job successes.

I, Tricia, learned this lesson the hard way. I was in a job that I enjoyed, but I also enjoyed all the extracurricular activities I was invited to participate in as part of a large organization. In addition to my full time engineering position, I led community service activities, was on the college recruiting team, and served as the point person for a national educational non-profit. All of these extra activities took a lot of time. Although they were valued by the organization, neither my manager nor my division received any credit for my leadership roles in these activities.

Since these efforts took time away from my core responsibilities, they appeared to reduce my direct contributions to my division – and that is exactly what my manager noted on my next performance review. Even though I had met my core job goals and had created value for my division, my extracurricular activities overshadowed my performance successes. I could have shifted the outcome of my performance review by paying more attention to my manager's priorities and drivers. I should have minimized communications about my extracurricular activities and focused on the core job responsibilities that my manager considered a top priority.

Mack was recruited to join a young company by a previous coworker he held in high regard. Serving as Area Manager, Mack enjoyed a wonderful position as a high achiever with a lot of freedom to grow his section of the business. As the company grew, financial pressures shifted the focus from long-term to short-term financial goals. Mack began to notice that the people around him often reacted in a variety of different ways to these financial pressures. Sometimes policies would be shifted to meet financial objectives or goals were altered to reward someone who might otherwise have not received their bonus. Since most of these decisions didn't directly have an impact on Mack or his growing business, he had not paid much attention to what his counterparts and senior management were altering to make things work for others. He did not pay attention to the shifting priorities and motivations of his organization and senior managers.

After several years of successes, the growth in Mack's area slowed and his short term financial performance fell. He was not willing to employ some of the techniques the other managers had engaged to make the short-term numbers look better than they actually were. Mack's performance review reflected his lack of willingness to cooperate. The shift in priorities that separated Mack and senior management did not happen overnight. Mack had seen the signs, but had not made the connection to how it would impact him should his business situation change.

Be aware of shifting organizational priorities and motivations and reflect on how they may impact your work environment.

A partner at an environmental consulting firm, Patrick interviewed a college senior for an entry-level position and was suddenly struck with memories of himself at that age. As Patrick listened to the candidate talk about wanting to work for a company that would always 'do the right thing' and about this young person's perceptions of 'the right thing,' he heard himself speaking those same words almost 20 years ago.

The reality of corporate culture, business expectations and what can technically be accomplished had greatly altered Patrick's perception of what it means to 'do the right thing.' Patrick still holds that as a primary motivation of his work; however, his lesson that day was that even when motivations remain the same, our experiences can lead us to a different understanding of how our motivations can be executed.

Coincidently, Patrick was being challenged with a manager who seemed to have a very different understanding of 'doing the right thing' than Patrick did. As Patrick drove back to the office from the interview, he contemplated his performance review which was anticipated the next quarter. Patrick decided that he needed to pay closer attention to his manager's motivations and close the gap with his own motivations before his next performance review.

Determine how your motivations may be more alike than different and how to connect to your manager's motivations or priorities.

Category 3: Your Organization's Priorities Are Not the Same as Yours

Perhaps your organization highly prioritizes profits while your top priority is flexibility in the workplace. These may seem out of whack, but if the company wants great employees, it may allow for flexibility to retain employees. The challenge is how to align what your organization prioritizes in your communications throughout the performance review process. For example, if your organization is focused on becoming a technology leader, be sure to regularly communicate your contributions to advancing technology. If your organization is primarily focused on generating profits, share how you contribute to increased sales or reduced expenditures.

If your organization's priorities are not the same as yours and there are no parallel priorities, it might be necessary to evaluate the type of organization you work for and consider where you can align what you value in the workplace. Although it would be nice to have it all, we can rarely have it all at one time. If your organization's priorities are far removed from yours and there is no alignment, it may be time to investigate other options.

I, Danielle, was in this situation for a brief period of time. I decided to accept a position outside of my industry because I thought I needed a change. It only took 30 days for me to realize that I had made a mistake by jumping into a position that had very different workplace priorities. After 60 days, I found a new job. Sometimes we make bad decisions, but the sooner we recognize it, the better off we are. Working through these exercises regularly reminds me of how important it is to find an environment that aligns with my priorities.

Difficult situations are a part of most people's workplace at some point in their career. When you encounter a difficult situation, you must determine the best solution for your work environment. Consult your networks, your personal board of directors (discussed later in Chapter 12) for guidance and verification of your proposed solution.

Category 4: Your Manager's and Your Organization's Priorities Are Not Aligned

One of the best pieces of advice we've ever heard is, "always stop and think: what else could be true?" View a conflict in priorities between your manager and your organization as an opportunity to expand your knowledge about people and excel in all environments. If you think your manager's priorities are in conflict with the organization's priorities, your challenge is to find a balance where you can align with both in a strategic way so as to avoid the conflict yourself. For example, if your manager is focused solely on advancing to the next level, he or she may be in conflict with the organization's goal of developing all employees to their greatest potential. Your job is to find a way to make your manager shine while still highlighting your personal accomplishments.

What you consider a high priority today and what you highly prioritize in five years will often be very different. The same goes for your organization and your manager, so periodically reflecting on priorities from all angles is imperative. Regardless of how your priorities align with your organization's or your manager's, understanding the factors driving business decisions enables you to align your communications and to *Exceed Expectations*.

SUCCESS STRATEGY: Determining Others Motives

Sometimes people feel that they are being targeted with negative feedback or being left out of good opportunities. Don't just assume that someone is "out to get you." There are often many other possibilities if you step back from the situation:

- Lack of effective communication
- You haven't proven your skills yet
- You are a new member of a long-functioning team
- People don't think that you want to be a part of the team
- Personality conflict that needs to be overcome

Every situation has two sides. Make sure you understand the full picture. It never hurts to simply ask someone why you are being left out. Take the feedback positively, not defensively and use the new information to alter your situation.

Zoey was a recent graduate hired as a buyer at the corporate office of a retail chain. She had great aspirations for her career and fabulous new ideas for her team. Zoey's boss had been with the retailer for many years and was nearing retirement. Zoey was crushed when she realized that her boss seemed to be motivated to keep everything moving along at the same pace, in the same way, with few changes and little innovation.

At the same time, the retailer had introduced a new advertising campaign that was greatly shifting the direction of the company. This campaign definitely appeared to be more aligned with Zoey's motivations than her boss'. Zoey's boss, motivated by the status quo, became a roadblock to her team's progress and her individual goals. Zoey had to find a way to succeed in her current position and shine in the new organization even though her boss wanted things to progress as easily and unchanged as possible. Zoey learned to provide her boss with all the information needed to demonstrate her accomplishments and how they aligned with job performance goals. She essentially gave her boss the content to complete the performance review form. It was no surprise when Zoey received *Exceeds Expectations*, was promoted and was then able to display her new ideas and innovation. Her new manager was very impressed with how Zoey had demonstrated success aligned with corporate goals.

Be flexible to find the solution that works for your particular situation – be creative, thorough and follow through.

Chapter 4 Takeaways

Explore Workplace Priorities

- Use the alignments you identify to communicate accomplishments that are valued by your manager and in your workplace.

- Motivations and priorities may shift over your career. Pay attention to your current work priorities and share changes with your manager.

- Be aware of shifting organizational priorities and motivations and reflect on how they may impact your work environment.

- Determine how your motivations may be more alike than different and how to connect to your manager's motivations or priorities.

- Be flexible to find the solution that works for your particular situation – be creative, thorough and follow through.

CHAPTER 5

Explore External Performance Review Influences

"Call it a clan, call it a network, call it a tribe, call it a family: Whatever you call it, whoever you are, you need one."

Jane Howard, Journalist and Writer

Just as the internal work environment influences the performance review process, the external environment can influence your communications and strategies for success, your review, and your ratings. Your external network can serve as a sounding board and provide the support, insight and assistance you need to *Exceed Expectations* within your organization. But, understand the state of your industry and those connected to your organization – your competitors, vendors and customers – are also important. The external perspective can help guide your strategic communications regarding your performance and lead you toward success.

Your External Networks

Having an external network of peers with whom you can share experiences, compare notes and discuss communication approaches is useful. Your network outside your organization can confirm that your performance review process experience is reasonable and can provide needed feedback on how to handle situations that may arise. Just remember we live in a small and extremely connected world – be careful about negative or destructive comments about your coworkers, managers or organization.

ACTION BOX 12: Examine Your External Network

Who do you turn to for career advice?

Example: My mother who is an HR Director at another company; Al Washington, a former manager; Dennis Walker, my best friend from college

---

Think about who is in your external network. Capture the people you turn to for career advice in **Action Box 12**.

I, Tricia, often bounce ideas and feedback I have received off of Danielle and other peers outside of my workplace. Since they don't know the people I work with or my organizational environment, they can provide objective suggestions and observations. They can also share how similar situations have played out in their organizations. This provides me with ideas of how to modify my approach, suggest changes, or adapt within my own organization.

Designate time each week to networking. Follow-up with contacts you've met, reconnect with past colleagues, or reach out to new networks. Spend just 5 percent of your week – that's just 2 hours a week – on networking and your network will expand exponentially. Build relationships or reconnect with colleagues from college, professional groups or events you have attended. Get involved in external activities within your industry or profession.

I, Danielle, continually use my external network to gauge my reactions to situations. I have a small group of people I rely on to provide me with honest and realistic feedback. Many years ago, I thought I was doing a great job of communicating my accomplishments throughout the year to my manager. I sent my manager monthly reports via email. I was grateful for my external network when at dinner one night, several peers asked if my manager read the reports I sent. I had never checked on that before. After talking with his secretary, I learned that he doesn't read attachments to email. He never read my monthly reports. I also learned he did read hard copies of information when traveling. From that point forward, I printed concise updates on my work and performance, and placed them on his mail pile. I knew these had a much better chance of making it into his briefcase, to be read with his mail while traveling. I appreciated that process check with my external network. It saved me from a potentially difficult performance review situation.

State of Your Industry

Read and network to stay connected to the latest information on your industry. Read trade publications, industry blogs and company press releases. Join trade or industry associations and read their newsletters or notices. Attend industry meetings and conferences to listen, learn and network with others who have insights to the current state and future directions of the industry.

Is your industry strong, thriving and growing? Is your industry in a downturn where layoffs are eminent or already widespread? Understanding the state of your industry can help you understand how to strategically communicate your performance with realistic expectations of your opportunities. For example, if your industry is in a downturn, heading into a performance review seeking a bonus, increased professional development opportunities or other benefits may indicate to your manager you are not in tune with your business environment. However, heading into the same downturn-era review with examples of how you have contributed to cost savings or added value to your organization may bump you up in ranking.

You don't want to become the expert in cassette tape technology when the industry is already digital and wireless. It is important to understand where your industry and organization are headed in the future. By keeping an eye on your industry's future, you can ensure you align communications with a forward view and maintain the skills you need to succeed.

Competitors, Vendors and Customers

If you are staying in tune with the state of your industry, you will be aware of the state of your competitors, vendors and customers. Who are your organization's competitors, vendors and customers? Do the competitors have employees in similar positions as you? Do your vendors or customers provide feedback to your manager regarding your performance? Understanding the competition and the opportunities they offer their employees, their reward systems, their mission and goals, and their state in the industry may help you position your communications or performance review conversations.

Subscribe to competitor's job postings or take note of skill sets valued in positions similar to yours. Industry publications may provide insight into strengths and weaknesses, internal processes and future directions. Understanding how vendors and customers play into your performance review can help you create a strategy to build better relationships, develop feedback mechanisms and impact the flow of information about your performance. Review or find out about any process by which your organization collects feedback from vendors and customers.

In a previous sales position, I, Danielle, suggested that we begin to survey our customers regarding their experience with our staff. Although the sales staff was the direct point of contact, a customer could interact with at least five other employees with every transaction. We had an annual communication to our customers already established, so adding a survey was easy. It became the salesperson's responsibility to ensure all customer surveys were returned to our manager. I used this opportunity to hand deliver the surveys to my customers and ensure that they were completed and returned directly to me. This became a great avenue for me to collect compliments from customers regarding my performance. It also gave me some improvement areas to quickly address. People like to be asked for their opinion, as long as it is accepted politely and acted upon. I made sure I addressed every comment provided by a customer and demonstrated these and my subsequent sales results in my performance review.

I, Tricia, stay connected to competitors so I can gauge how my program is doing. It has proven personally beneficial as I have advanced in my professional role. Several years ago, I was elected

> **SUCCESS STRATEGY: Interacting with Vendors or Customers**
>
> Very few positions within large corporations have direct contact with vendors or customers. Express an interest in getting to know some of your organization's vendors or customers by asking to participate in meetings as a learning experience. Establish an external network with your organization's competitors, vendors and customers in the same way you work on your personal external network. Through professional organizations and industry events, take time to expand your network to include people from each of these areas. Seek them out, sit next to people you don't know, follow up with them and slowly build a professional relationship that ultimately expands your own external network.

to the board of a national organization that brought valued recognition to my institution. A colleague at a peer institution, a competitor in the academic world, shared the items she negotiated when she was elected to the same board. I was able to leverage my knowledge of her negotiated items (travel expenses, discretionary funds and student staff support) to secure an even better package. Having information and understanding of what the competition was offering allowed me to receive the support I needed and positive recognition of my board contributions on my performance review.

External Comparisons

Once you understand your external work environment, you will be better prepared to clearly and effectively communicate how your successes provide value to your organization. By taking time to understand the external environment, you also gain information to use in the review process, or an external comparison.

Answer these key questions for additional understanding of your external environment.

Is your salary in line with others in your industry, experience level, job category, and/or geographic area? If not, having the data can provide the background required for a discussion with your manager. The most reliable way of determining salary data that is specific to you is to build relationships with recruiters in your field. They can give you real-time and geographic data on which positions are available, salary expectations, and skill sets needed. Find industry recruiters who are looking to build relationships with people just like you through industry meetings, trade magazines, professional organizations and job posting sites.

Are your goals and expectations in line with those of others in your industry, experience level, job category, and/or geographic area? If not, understanding where others are headed can guide your path or provide the data needed for a discussion on your career path with your manager. It can provide information for academic goals and professional networks and the return on investment for your company funding such opportunities or professional associations.

Does your external network involve customers and contribute to your success? If so, can you turn your network into an opportunity to excel for your performance review? You can highlight personal relationships that could become customer relationships. You can offer external information or feedback on a product or service that seems unsuccessful.

How does your organization measure up? Is your company an industry leader? An emerging player? The company everyone wants to work for? Respected in the industry? Your network can give you a feel for all of these issues. With this information, you can more meaningfully contribute to your organization's success and convey your knowledge during your review with strategic improvements.

Where is the industry headed? Is it in the same direction as your organization? Provide information to your manager about the direction you would like to head and how it aligns with the path your organization is taking. Position yourself to be a part of your industry and organization's future.

What are the backgrounds of leaders at other organizations? Are they similar to the backgrounds at your organization? How does your background compare? What experiences need to be in your future? Use this information to set personal and organizational goals and to request training during your performance review. Highlighting the skills you already have or may be gaining through training may open opportunities and ensure you maintain a high-ranking status. Your company should also value this because it can limit the need to hire others with the skills desired.

Which departments in other organizations are hiring and which ones are reducing headcounts? Are your areas of expertise in the growing or shrinking areas? Which skills should you develop to remain relevant? Bring these up in your performance review.

Are you connected to job opportunities in your field and your organization? These can help you understand your position within the marketplace as well as the value you provide to your organization. Perusing job descriptions can provide useful insights into the skills and abilities desired of today's top recruits, and can highlight areas where you may need to retool or refresh.

I, Danielle, had a manager early in my career who told me she read the classified job ads every Sunday in the newspaper. I couldn't understand why someone who appeared to be happy in her position was always looking for something else. I soon realized that she used the job postings to decipher information about our competitors. If they were hiring, there must be a big project coming up. If postings in our field tapered off, the industry was slowing down and we needed to step up our marketing efforts. Even if advertisements did not include the company name, she often knew who had posted the ad because of the fax number or email address listed for resume responses. To this day, I always read the classified ads in industry publications to see how companies are doing. Sometimes I find out that my own company is hiring for a position I had not heard about. This has become valuable information throughout my career.

After evaluating your external environment, think about additional people who could offer advice and information that would help you *Exceed Expectations*. If a specific name comes to mind, note it in **Action Box 13**, or capture the skills of people you need to add to your external network.

The Strategies Grid focuses on your current job responsibilities that are influenced and affected by your internal and external environments. Your insights and understanding of your environment will help you create a strategic Performance Review Action Plan (Chapter 14) and will influence how you complete the Strategies Grid as we move through the remaining chapters.

ACTION BOX 13: Identify External Network Needs

What are the valued skills of people you need to add to your external network?

Example: An excellent networker; A recruiter who can keep me posted on jobs in my industry; A customer who can fill me in on competitor products

Chapter 5 Takeaways

Explore External Performance Review Influences

- Knowing the state of your industry and understanding how others perceive your organization give you valuable information to use in your performance review.

- External networks provide an outsider perspective on situations you encounter.

- Competitors, vendors, and customers can and often do influence your performance review.

- Compare your workplace to others in your industry to gain a realistic perspective of your personal situation and what other opportunities are available.

CHAPTER 6

Define Performance Review Success

"The secret of success is sincerity.
Once you can fake that you've got it made."

Jean Giraudoux, French Novelist

My definition of performance review success is likely different from yours. For me, Tricia, success includes doing the best I can do and making a difference every day through my work. Performance review success for me means *Exceeding Expectations* in all my job responsibilities and ensuring my management knows and values all that my program and staff accomplishes. But success to my manager and my organization may look very different. Performance review success for one of my previous managers was simply completing the review process, not providing useful feedback to employees or assisting with career development.

Defining what a successful performance review looks like and what it accomplishes are important steps in the performance review process. The challenge is that a successful performance review may have a different definition for you than for your manager or your organization. Taking time to define performance review success from all angles will enable you to approach the process in a manner that keeps your definition of success in the forefront.

Success for You

For many of us, the performance review has become one of our routine yearly tasks. It will be done, whether you like it or not, and the process may be uncomfortable and unclear. Many of us may view it as a waste of time and something our manager must simply check off the list and mark as complete. Success for you, until now, may simply have been defined as surviving the performance review process.

If we view the performance review process from the Balanced Model and work within an employee driven process – a process where YOU take the lead for your own performance review – then you can aim for a different vision of success. You can aim for your definition of success and drive the process so that your goals have

In Trevor's first performance review as a senior manager, he was determined to be prepared when he met with his new manager. He had gathered and documented concrete examples of his success for every metric outlined on the corporate form and examples for a few metrics he added to demonstrate other areas of accomplishment. Trevor was also careful to include areas where he knew he needed improvement and used these as an avenue to introduce training and conferences he wanted to attend to strengthen his skills. Trevor defined success as being prepared for anything that would come up in the review.

As Trevor's manager provided feedback, Trevor was able to share the examples he had prepared and fill in the gaps in areas where his manager had not personally observed his performance. This led to some shifts in Trevor's rating on the form his manager had originally completed. As Trevor left the review, his manager told him that he had never negotiated a performance review before. Trevor's manager was very impressed with how prepared he was for the meeting. That was exactly what Trevor wanted to hear. He was happy his review was successful.

Know your definition of success.

a better chance of being met before, during and after the performance review.

Imagine what a successful performance review would look like for you. When you walk out the door of your performance review location, what will have happened for you to define your review as successful? Perhaps success is getting the raise, promotion, responsibility or recognition that you feel you deserve. Perhaps it is having a better defined and supported plan for your career path. Perhaps it is an opportunity to develop skills that will help you move closer toward your career goals. Your personal success may include any of the following factors:

- Support for your career path plan

- A promotion

- A raise

- Added responsibility

- Modified responsibility

- Recognition

- Support for training and development

- Defined goals

- Feedback on goals and/or performance

- Performance improvement areas defined

- An exit strategy

- Information gathering and/or sharing

- Relief with review completion

- An established method for future feedback

Use **Action Box 14** to define a successful performance review for you.

ACTION BOX 14: Describe Your Idea of Performance Review Success

My performance review is successful for me when:

Example: I get the raise I deserve; I understand training options for the next year; My manager understands what I have accomplished

---

Your measures of performance review success may change from year to year as your career goals and situations change. Being aware of your current situation and the measures of success you have defined can help you determine the way you present your accomplishments, the questions to ask in your review or the communications you may need to have before and after your review.

Success for Your Manager

Now consider what a successful performance review looks like for your manager. What are your manager's objectives or expected outcomes of the performance review process? Different managers have different styles and vary widely in their desire and abilities to provide valuable feedback during a performance review. Your organization may have strict procedures to follow for the performance review with a set form, boxes to check, set ratings to dole-out and comments to fill in. Or, perhaps your manager follows a more fluid conversational process to provide feedback without standardized forms and rankings. Each of these styles indicates what a successful performance review looks like for your manager. Success measures for your manager may include:

- Fulfill requirements of the organization
- Determine how raises or bonuses will be distributed
- Understand each employee's motivations, values and/or priorities
- Understand each employee's career desires
- Build management skills
- Document what is already known or learn more about each employee
- Develop metrics for the next fiscal year
- Structure budgets for the next fiscal year

- Identify needs for the next fiscal year

- Create or restructure project teams or staff for the next fiscal year

- Allocate promotions and responsibilities for the next fiscal year

Use **Action Box 15** to define what a successful performance review looks like for your manager. If you have multiple managers, complete this exercise for each one. If you are not sure what success looks like for your manager, ask your manager directly or collect information from those who have gone through the process with your manager in the past.

ACTION BOX 15: Define Your Manager's Performance Review Success

My performance review is successful for my manager(s) when:

Example: It is over in less than 10 minutes; I understand what is expected of me over the next year; He is updated on my projects

---

When your manager's definition of performance review success doesn't match yours, you have to balance your personal goals with your manager's goals. You need to strategically align to your manager's definition of success. If your success requires getting recognition or feedback, be sure to facilitate the discussion so it is easier for you to do that. But don't let your manager off the hook; don't let him or her bail out of the process to just get it over with.

For Walter's manager, performance review success is when all reviews are completed on time. Walter's manager wants to spend as little time as possible on the process, and just really wants to get it done so that he can check it off his to-do list. Walter knew this coming into the group and determined that he needed to make things as easy as possible for his manager.

Walter has made a tradition of scheduling his review as early in the cycle as possible, and of providing his manager all the information he needs to complete the form well in advance of the review. Walter provides the information electronically and in the same format as his corporate performance review form so his manager can just copy and paste the information into the form. Walter is making it really easy for his manager and regularly receives an outstanding rating.

**Keep it simple when possible
– make success easy for your manager.**

Understanding success for your manager gives you information to adjust your communications and performance review expectations. One of your goals is to make the process as easy as possible for your manager. For example, if your manager spends a lot of time and effort writing thorough reviews for each employee, then provide all the necessary data early in the process so that your review is one of the first written and includes data you have supplied. If your manager uses the performance review to report bonuses or promotions, communicate your accomplishments well in advance of your review meeting. If your manager simply fills out the form during the review meeting, having recently communicated your relevant successes keeps those results on the forefront. It is just as difficult for your manager to remember what you achieved six months ago and it is for you.

Let's explore various manager success factors and suggested techniques for your performance review and communications with your manager. You may have more than one manager or more than one person who will have input on your performance review. Take this into consideration and make sure your communications reach everyone effectively. You may use this suggested verbiage when communicating to your manager, but as always, be sure to customize it to align with your situation.

For each manager success factor below, consider the tips and suggested verbiage to strategically respond to your manager:

Fulfill requirements of the organization

Make his or her job easy. Use the company performance review form as a guideline and provide your manager with detailed accomplishments that demonstrate *Exceeding Expectations* in each area.

> *I compiled a list of successes from the past year to assist in the performance review process.*

Determine how raises or bonuses will be distributed

Since raises are often calculated from a pool of available money, the ranking of employees will likely impact this determination. Giving your manager concrete evidence of how you have excelled will give him or her the ability to rank you higher than your coworkers.

> *In preparation for the upcoming performance review, I gathered some successes from the past year.*

Since bonuses are often calculated against pre-set metrics, evidence of meeting or exceeding these metrics will allow your manager to reward you as planned. Also remember that bonuses often come from a pool of available money and you may be competing with others for the same money.

As part of my team's end-of-the-year review process, we gauge our performance against metrics and goals for the year. We were very excited to celebrate surpassing the metrics the company set for our team.

Understand each employee's motivations, values and/or priorities

Share your story! There is a fine line between personal and professional information to be shared in the workplace. Veering too far in either direction will create challenges. The first step is for you to understand what you value and then share your current and future job related motivations, values and/or priorities with your manager as appropriate.

I enjoy working in an environment that recognizes me for making a difference. I hope to continue using my technical and professional skills to advance in our organization.

Understand each employee's career desires

Many managers want to develop their employees. The first step is for you to understand what your career desires are. Effective communication of these desires is just as important. You don't want to come across as cocky, or miss the mark and not communicate your desires at all. Finding the right balance between these is critical.

I really enjoy international travel and would welcome an opportunity for an assignment oversees.

Build management skills

Provide opportunities for your manager to provide you with feedback or guidance. If your desire is to move into management or into a higher level of management, ask your manager to describe how he or she has honed skills or to suggest training for you...and then share what you learn with your manager.

I need some feedback. I am interested in moving into a management position later in my career. Can you share with me ways I might start to develop some of the skills I'll need to succeed in this type of role?

Document what is already known or learn more about each employee

Sharing personal information may be very uncomfortable, but it is a necessary part of the workplace. Developing relationships with people requires sharing personal information. Determine what you are willing to share and find a comfortable way to develop a deeper relationship.

It was a beautiful weekend. We rode our bikes to a local restaurant for dinner on Saturday night. The kids really enjoyed it.

Develop metrics for the next fiscal year

Develop your own metrics for the upcoming year and present them to your manager. Being prepared and ahead of the curve will certainly impress your manager.

I was considering the workload for next year and have developed milestones that reflect the corporate goals.

Structure budgets for the next fiscal year

Develop your own budget for the portion of the business you manage. You may not think you manage a portion of your organization's business, but we all manage income and expenses of our organization. Consider travel expenses, attendance at conferences, marketing materials, copies and prints, using resources that may not be necessary, etc. Present a return on investment for your goals and proposed training.

> *As I was reviewing last year's budget successes, I set budget goals for the upcoming year.*

Identify needs for the next fiscal year

Develop your own resource needs. Every employee uses resources. Consider training, equipment, personnel assistance, marketing assistance, external resources, etc.

> *I am proud of how efficient our team has been this year. To achieve the same success next year, we need 2 additional programmers and I need to hone my skills in XYZ software. Training classes are available at the Software National Conference in May.*

Create or restructure project teams or staff for the next fiscal year

Determine which project team or project you want to work on and communicate that information with valid reasons for your desires.

> *The ABC project looks like an exciting opportunity to use the skills I've developed and provide an opportunity to learn X, Y, and Z from Jack Johnson.*

Allocate promotions and responsibilities for the next fiscal year

Determine which responsibilities you'd like to take on and communicate why you are the right person to manage that responsibility.

We've talked about expanding the corporate recruiting process in the future. I've developed some great ideas and would like to spearhead those efforts.

Determine what promotion possibilities are available within your organization and which skill-sets are needed in each position. Provide concrete evidence to demonstrate your qualifications for the position you want.

I understand that the supervisor role in the plastics group will be open next quarter. This position would be an excellent fit in my career progression plan, allowing me to use the financial, management and marketing skills I've developed.

Success for Your Organization

Companies and organizations conduct performance reviews for a variety of reasons. Perhaps your organization conducts performance reviews to ensure annual documentation on employee performance for raises, bonuses, promotions or layoffs. Organizations surely want to protect themselves from unlawful termination or discrimination lawsuits and performance reviews provide needed documentation. Or perhaps your organization uses performance reviews to guide succession planning or employee development. By understanding the goals of your organization and how your organization views success for the performance review, you can modify your approach to the process, or better understand where your review fits into the larger organizational structure and goals.

Use **Action Box 16** to define your understanding of your organization's view of a successful performance review process. Once again, if you're not sure what these are, discuss it with your manager or others within your organization who have gone through the process before or have insight into your organization.

ACTION BOX 16: Define Your Organization's Performance Review Success

My performance review is successful for my organization when:

Example: It is completed on time; My successes and challenges are documented

I, Danielle, have shifted companies several times in my career. It takes keen observation and effort to determine what a company values in the performance review process. Since the best information comes from having been through the process, I tend to find someone who has been with the company for a long period of time. They can give me tips and are generally anxious to share their experiences.

Once you have an understanding of your organization's definition of performance review success, you can strategically align to it in your preparation and communications regarding your own performance review.

At this point, you should have a much better understanding of your roles and responsibilities, as well as the performance review process and the factors that influence the process and its success. Knowledge truly is power in the case of the performance review process. And knowledge about yourself is empowering. The more you know and understand, the better your ability to be strategic in your communications and responsibilities. The more strategic you can be, the easier it is for you to *Exceed Expectations*.

Organizational Success Factors and Your Strategic Response

If your organization uses performance reviews for...	Then...
Legal purposes	Be prepared with your own documentation of your performance and keep copies for your records.
Variable pay based on performance	Showcase how you provide value and *Exceed Expectations* to maximize your pay potential.
Promotion and advancement opportunities	Communicate your career goals to your manager and be sure your performance review and the documents you share showcase how you are poised to advance to the next level.
Career development	Communicate your career goals to your manager and be sure your performance review reflects your next steps or provides guidance on development opportunities for the next year.
Maintaining programs expected by employees	Take advantage of the system and ensure your personnel file includes examples of accomplishments and successes.

Chapter 6 Takeaways

Define Performance Review Success

- Performance review success is different for everyone. Know your definition of success.

- Knowledge is power in the performance review and knowledge about yourself is empowering.

- Defining what performance review success means for you, your manager, and your organization allows you to align goals and communicate the right message.

- Keep it simple when possible – make success easy for your manager.

Understand Job Responsibilities

Strategies Grid

Strategy 1	Strategy 2	Strategy 3	Strategy 4	Strategy 5
Job Responsibilities	Goals or Objectives	Accomplishments	Challenges	Success Methods

The first strategy in our Balanced Performance Review Model is to define your job responsibilities and understand them in the context of your organization's performance review process. We often jump right into the performance review, without taking the time to understand our role, what we are being evaluated on and the motivations for the performance review within our organization. Taking this first step allows you to be strategic throughout the entire performance review process. In earlier chapters you identified and defined your organization's performance review process, workplace priorities, external influences, and success factors. The next step is clearly defining your job.

CHAPTER 7

Define Your Job

"It's not the hours you put in your work that counts, it's the work you put in the hours."

Sam Ewing, Author

What is your official job description? We all know what we do on a daily basis, but how does that fit into the expectations of your manager and organization? Most people do a lot more than the specific tasks outlined in the original job posting, official job description, or performance review. Before you can communicate how effectively you are doing your job, you need to define your job and be in agreement with your manager on the expectations. Once you are clear about your job responsibilities and expectations, you can begin to collect accomplishments, market yourself year round, and demonstrate that you *Exceed Expectations* in those areas valued for your position. The Strategies Grid should help you focus on excelling in your current job by providing the means to better understand and communicate your job responsibilities and expectations.

Locate your official job description if one is available. Some organizations are diligent about developing and updating these for each position. You may easily find it online, in your original job posting, or through some other internal job classification system. Other organizations may leave it up to the manager to define roles or use the performance review form and annual review process to track and manage job responsibilities. You may not even have a job description and simply follow the lead of others as to what you should be working on next. If you have an official job description, it may only provide a vague listing of job responsibilities and broad phrasing to cover a number of tasks. Regardless of how your organization operates, identify those publicly documented and identified responsibilities that may or may not be a part of your actual day-to-day work. Use **Action Box 17** to compile these official job responsibilities.

Do your current day-to-day responsibilities match what you have written in Action Box 17? What does your true current job description look like? Identify all additional job responsibilities, expertise or authority. Compile them in **Action Box 18** to build on,

---

ACTION BOX 17: List Your Official Job Responsibilities

Example: Monthly project reports to region manager; Market services to potential customers; Report to work daily with a good attitude
1.
2.
3.
4.
5.

---

or redefine, your official job description. Begin by brainstorming your daily tasks. Using your daily tasks and official job description, draft your current job responsibilities. Your current job responsibilities should reflect what you **actually do** and **are responsible for** today. This should not be a high-level overview like you might put on a resume, but a detailed look at what you truly do as a contributor to your organization. Quantify your job responsibilities when possible, using measurable descriptions such as:

- Manage x # employees
- Sell x tons or x $ of product
- Responsible for x product lines
- Support x # of customers
- Manage operating budget of x $ millions annually
- Produce x # reports per year
- Write x proposals per year

ACTION BOX 18: Write Your Current Job Responsibilities

Use your daily tasks to write your current job responsibilities.

Daily Tasks Brainstorm	Current Job Responsibilities
Example: Answer customer calls; Edit reports for manager; Handle all customer billing complaints	*Example: Manage interaction and billing issues for 125 customers; Review an average of 5 documents per week for accuracy*

As an example, if your daily tasks are returning customer calls, reviewing customer accounts for billing errors, tracking product deliveries and following up with the sales team on product orders, then your job description could include: 1) support 3 sales people; 2) manage customer billing issues for 140 accounts; and 3) maintain positive customer relations with over 75 customers.

Job responsibilities often morph over time, perhaps shrinking, expanding and blending as opportunities arise and organizations change. While your manager may define and document your core job responsibilities, there are often "other duties as assigned" that can accumulate and take up a significant part of your work day. I, Tricia, have presented my Strategies Grid in a performance review and found that my manager did not realize I was still engaged in an extra responsibility no longer core to our changing business. Documenting all my job responsibilities and providing information on my accomplishments and challenges allowed my manager to shift some of my responsibilities, which allowed me to focus on core business needs. To *Exceed Expectations,* you need to clearly define and communicate all job responsibilities, and have them documented in the Strategies Grid.

Strategic Job Responsibilities

Now that you have defined and quantified your daily tasks and current job responsibilities, it is time to think about your job strategically. Every organization has a mission, strategic plan and/or overarching goals driving it forward. A strategic job description ties what you do in your day-to-day job to the goals of your organization. It demonstrates the connection points, visible value and organizational goal alignment you and your job provide. It demonstrates that you have aligned accomplishments, are capable of doing your job and are engaged in the success of your organization through your position. By connecting the dots between your job description and job responsibilities, you demonstrate how your work contributes to the organization's goals, the value you provide.

Identify your organization's goals and/or mission in **Action Box 19**. It may be challenging to find the goals or mission of your organization, department or team. Try exploring your organization's website or sales, marketing or recruiting information. You may identify goals at various levels throughout your organization that tie back to you and your responsibilities.

Given your organization's goals and/or mission in Action Box 19, strategize your job description and job responsibilities. Show you are an integral part of your organization's success, as in the examples provided. Rewrite your job responsibilities to provide focus and goal alignment that are absent in your more generic, original job description. This makes it easier to showcase how your performance *Exceeds Expectations* and provides a means to establish clear communications with your manager about the alignment of your responsibilities.

ACTION BOX 19: Define Your Organization's Goals and/or Mission

Example: To provide superior training to professionals seeking to increase their workplace success and achieve their career goals.

Current vs. Strategic Job Responsibility Examples

Current Job Responsibility	Strategic Job Responsibility
Oversee and administer the day-to-day operations of a $3 million division	Manage operations of a $3 million division within budget and in accordance with organizational goals
Build 30 new relationships	Develop 30 strategic partnerships to expand market share
Represent the organization at six national conferences and events	Advance the organization's reputation and technology leadership by participating in and presenting at six national conferences and events
Provide technical assistance to over 75 customers	Be identified as a technology expert while providing technical assistance to over 75 customers
Other duties as assigned	Edit an average of 10 reports a week for accuracy and professionalism
	Receive calls from 20 customers a week and take care of billing issues to ensure timely payment and excellent customer relationships
	Manage 5 trade show marketing events to increase exposure and reputation of company

So, how do you rewrite your job responsibilities into strategic job responsibilities? Focus on incorporating measurable accomplishments. You are simply taking a more generic phrasing of your job responsibility and making it more specific, focused, and goal related. Change the job responsibility from a passive statement to an active statement. Review your organization's goals that were identified in Action Box 19 and incorporate the same language in your strategic job responsibility. If your organization is focused on exceptional service, include those words and/or metrics to demonstrate that you provide exceptional service through your current responsibilities.

'Other duties as assigned' is a tricky and ambiguous addition to a lot of job descriptions. Try to identify specifically what this means for your position. Although it can change dramatically over time, identify those extra duties you have been responsible for over the past year and foresee for the coming year.

Use **Action Box 20** to rewrite the job responsibilities you identified in Action Boxes 17 (Official Job Responsibilities) and 18 (Current Job Responsibilities) into strategic job responsibilities. Align these with your organization's goals and/or mission described in Action Box 19 (Organization Goals).

Use your strategic job responsibilities from **Action Box 20** to populate the first column of your Strategies Grid.

ACTION BOX 20: Rewrite to Identify Strategic Job Responsibilities

Rewrite your official and current job responsibilities into strategic job responsibilities. *Examples are provided on page 99.*

Official/Current Job Responsibilities (Action Boxes 17 and 18)	Strategic Job Responsibilities

Strategies Grid

Strategy 1	Strategy 2	Strategy 3	Strategy 4	Strategy 5
Job Responsibilities	Goals or Objectives	Accomplishments	Challenges	Success Methods
1.				
2.				
3.				

Chapter 7 Takeaways

Define Your Job

- Job responsibilities should be strategic and align with your organization's goals and mission.

- Determine how your official job description differs from your actual day-to-day activities and communicate these differences to your manager.

- Demonstrate measureable goals and results in your strategic job description. Let your manager know exactly what you are accomplishing or working toward accomplishing.

Define Goals or Objectives

Strategies Grid

Strategy 1	Strategy 2	Strategy 3	Strategy 4	Strategy 5
Job Responsibilities	Goals or Objectives	Accomplishments	Challenges	Success Methods

The second strategy in our Balanced Performance Review Model is to define your goals and objectives. Defining goals is a process that most people start and never finish because they just don't know how to get there. The goals defined in Strategy 2 will tie directly to the job responsibilities detailed in Strategy 1 and should clearly define where you are headed.

We approach goal setting a bit differently than most. We start with a number of exercises that explore a bit about who you are – your likes and dislikes, strengths and weaknesses. This information will put you in the right mindset to define your goals. We then tie this understanding of the real you into exercises defining your lifetime goals, then five-year goals and finally finish with one-year goals and milestones. This may be the hardest strategy and the most challenging exercises to complete since goal setting is oftentimes not a favorite activity. But, by stepping back and investigating who you are and how your goals align with your job responsibilities, you understand your career directions and can better manage your performance review process.

As you move throughout your days, come back to these exercises as new ideas and insights come to light. You'll often be surprised by what you begin to notice about yourself and others in your daily activities.

CHAPTER 8

Reveal the Real You

"It is better to look ahead and prepare than to look back and regret."

Jackie Joyner-Kersee, Gold Medal Olympic Athlete

Successful people know exactly who they are: strengths, areas needing growth, where they are headed in life and how they are going to get there. If you don't understand **who** you are, you'll never understand **where** you are headed. Even successful people feel lost sometimes, but they regroup, regain focus and set new goals. We all contemplate the "what if" scenarios. If I never had to work for someone else again, what would my life look like? If I never had to worry about income, where would I live? If I won the lottery, what would I do with all that money? If I had my dream job, what would it look like?

The performance review process should be about the past (what you have done), the present (what you are doing now) and the future (what you should be doing and where you want to go). To take control of your performance review, you must understand where you want to be in the future. This includes not only envisioning your dream job, but also understanding your lifetime, shorter term goals, and the direction you want your career to head. By understanding your desired future and defining your goals, you can better position yourself in your performance review and in your organization to achieve exactly that.

At some point you have certainly thought about what you like and dislike about your job. You've considered strengths and weaknesses, or coworkers have complimented successes and, perhaps, commented about challenges. You may have considered other opportunities within your organization or environment. Considering all of these things in concert with each other provides great insight into your areas of expertise and your greatest opportunities to *Exceed Expectations*.

It is important to explore what you know about yourself and your environment as you head into a performance review. By taking stock of your abilities, the perceptions of those around you and the environment in which you work, you obtain the critical information you will need to *Exceed Expectations* in the workplace.

Writing this information down makes it real and enhances your ability to communicate your performance accomplishments effectively.

As you move throughout this chapter, consider how you may incorporate what you learn or what you share within the Action Boxes into the Strategies Grid. For example, your strengths will influence your goals or objectives for your job and your career. But they may also come into play as you strategically communicate your accomplishments, address challenges or implement success methods. Understanding the **real** you influences your performance review strategy. Your insights should be incorporated into the rest of the Strategies Grid.

Likes and Dislikes

Consider the aspects of your current job and previous jobs that you like and dislike. The things you do, the things you say, the jobs and tasks that attract and excite you, and the perks you receive will likely have some things in common. Exploring your likes and dislikes in the workplace helps provide a framework for better understanding both yourself and the environment in which you thrive.

I, Danielle, have what most people consider an odd like. I've noticed that all the jobs I have enjoyed have bottled water cooler dispensers available for employees. The jobs I haven't liked have not. It may just be a coincidence, but a bottled water cooler is something I look for in a workplace now. It has become a sign to me that my prospective employer has taken a small step to make things more convenient.

Exploring your likes and dislikes in your volunteer or extra-curricular settings can also be insightful in discovering areas you like or dislike that might not correlate with your current job. It gives more insight to which environments allow you to succeed.

Volunteer activities are generally managed differently from corporate activities. Non-profit or community organizations often have very different goals. These environments can either frustrate us or motivate us. Within volunteer or extracurricular settings, you are drawn to those situations, tasks, environments and people you like. If you didn't like the task, you would not be volunteering. We all need a variety of outlets to hone our skills, network and meet our personal needs. If you find that you are happier in your volunteer activities, your challenge is to examine how you can translate the likes from your volunteer roles to your job. For some people fulfillment is the extracurricular and a job is a means to an end. An example is someone who works hard and saves money so they can take a five year sabbatical to build houses in developing countries. How do your extracurricular activities play a part in your overall fulfillment?

Many years ago I, Tricia, was participating in a company training class designed to help employees map out their career goals and envision their future. The instructor took the class through a likes/dislikes exercise where we mapped them across various segments of our lives, such as work, family, volunteer, health, and school. The instructor then had us make a list of all the extracurricular activities in which we were involved. I was amazed at the length of my list: local grade school tutor, community service coordinator, community event coordinator, recruiter, sports club participant, graduate student, national conference committee chair, local math competition chair, and on and on. And then the instructor shared a bit of information I will never forget: "If you are not getting what you need at work, you will seek it elsewhere." I was seeking everything elsewhere. My likes were all outside of my job. It was eye opening! From that point forward, I used my performance review to move closer to my likes at work and eventually transitioned to a new career that seems like it is an extracurricular activity each and every day.

Once you understand your likes and dislikes, it is easier to direct your workplace communications and opportunities toward those aspects you like and enjoy. Keep in mind that likes and dislikes are not the same as strengths and weaknesses. You can be great at a task, but hate it. You can love a task, but be awful at it. Be open about what you like and dislike as you investigate your current job, previous jobs and volunteer or extracurricular activities. Use **Action Box 21** to list the likes and dislikes of your current and previous jobs. For your current position, define your likes and dislikes for your strategic job responsibilities.

Don't forget about the jobs you held as a teenager. I, Danielle, was a roller-skating car-hop at Sonic when I was in high school. I loved interacting with the customers. Now one of my favorite vacations each year is visiting a friend who owns an ice cream store. I love working at the ice cream store and talking with all the customers. This is very representative of my desire to interact with a variety of people every day. And it was apparent when I was 16 years old.

Strengths

One of the most dreaded and common interview questions is "What are your strengths and weaknesses?" If you have been through an interviewing workshop, you likely learned how to spin your weaknesses into strengths. Take a few minutes to really think about what your strengths are, not those weaknesses turned into strengths you use in an interview. What are you really good at? What can you do that *Exceeds Expectations* each and every time without much energy or thought.

We all have strengths in a variety of areas, perhaps physical, mental, analytical reasoning, verbal communication, or written communication. No strength is too small or too large when examining your career or preparing for your perormance review.

ACTION BOX 21: List Your Likes and Dislikes

List your likes and dislikes for each situation below. Use the Words to Spark Thoughts at the end of the book if you need more examples.

LIKES	DISLIKES
My Current Job and Strategic Job Responsibilities	
Example: Free coffee; Autonomy; Flexible schedule; Great commute; Great manager	*Example: Micromanagement; Long drive; No future; Lack of respect for coworkers*
My Previous Jobs	
Example: Great office; Free parking; Fun group of people; Bottled water	*Example: Expected to socialize too much with coworkers; Cubicle; Lack of diversity; No support*
My Volunteer or Extracurricular Activities	
Example: Feel like I make a difference; Great contacts; No pressure; Fun	*Example: Volunteer management; Too much drama; Bureaucracy; Paperwork; Can be demanding*

> **SUCCESS STRATEGY: Strengths in the Workplace**
>
> An easy way to determine what your manager thinks your strengths are is to look at what tasks you are assigned to perform. Start paying attention to the functions other people ask you to do. You are generally asked to repeat things that others perceive you do well.

Remember that strengths don't have to be something you enjoy; they just need to be what you do repeatedly well. Use **Action Box 22** to write down your strengths. The exercise is divided into three sections to help you clearly define different areas. If these categories don't seem relevant to you, choose others that do.

Are your strengths being used in your job? Does your manager have a good understanding of what you bring to the table? When you understand your strengths and how they align to your job responsibilities and the goals, values or priorities of your manager and organization, you can identify ways to showcase your strengths and communicate them. *Exceeding Expectations* on your performance review includes shining a light on all you have done well and ensuring your strengths are highlighted.

Use **Action Box 23** to align your strengths with your current strategic job responsibilities. You can also consider how they align with your desired next position, but remember that it may be important to be successful in your current position before you can move to the next one.

Compliments

Now that you've determined what you think your strengths are, let's consider what others observe about your strengths and skills. What kind of compliments do you consistently receive? Compliments give us a window into other people's view of our personal brand – that public view of who we are and what we are about.

ACTION BOX 22: Identify Your Strengths

Write your strengths in each of the categories listed below. If you are drawing a blank, use the Words to Spark Thoughts at the end of the book to stimulate your thoughts.

Personality or Character Strengths
Example: Loyal; Supportive; Mentoring; Empathetic; Caring

Training/Knowledge-Based/Learned Strengths
Example: Expert water analyzer; Financial modeling; Specific equipment that you can operate

Soft Skills Strengths
Example: Managing people; Conflict resolution; Public speaking; Negotiating

ACTION BOX 23: Align Your Strengths Strategically

How do your strengths align with your current strategic job responsibilities and performance expectations?

My Strength	Aligns with this Job Responsibility
Example: Excellent editor	Example: Proof all documents before sending

Which of these strengths are valued by your manager or organization?
Example: Organization; Editing Skills

Are any of these strengths measured on your performance evaluation?
Example: Organization skills are

How can you incorporate your strengths into the Strategies Grid?
Example: Highlight them in the accomplishments section

If you can't think of any compliments, begin to pay attention to what people say to you. Compliments come in a variety of forms; you might not recognize them until you look for them. The things we often consider to be easy skills are often the things that set us apart and make us exceptional. Compliments might be small, such as, "I enjoyed your presentation this morning." And they might be large, such as, "Your dedication inspires all of us. I am going to nominate you for employee of the month." People recognize others frequently, but most of us are too busy to notice. Start noticing when, why, and for what others recognize you. Some people choose not to hear compliments because they aren't happy with themselves. If this is you, stop and begin to really listen to what others say to you. You will often be surprised at how other's perceptions can change your own.

Use **Action Box 24** to list compliments you have received. Remember to include the small ones and the large ones. Understanding the compliments you receive is a large part of understanding how others perceive you. We have provided three categories for compliments to give you areas to think about. If these are not appropriate for your situation, select different categories.

Do the compliments you hear align with the strengths you listed in Action Box 22? Do they align with measures on your performance review? If they do, then you are effectively showcasing and using your strengths in the workplace. If they do not, explore ways you can showcase or communicate your strengths and successes to generate compliments or other feedback.

Does your manager hear about the compliments you receive? He should! One easy way to do this via email is to reply to the sender, thanking the sender for the kind words and copying your manager. Collecting compliments and compiling them to share in your performance review can also be effective in reaching that *Exceeds Expectations* rating, but don't overdo it. Once a quarter in a concise email is effective while 18 random emails won't work as

ACTION BOX 24: List Compliments

List the compliments you receive in each of the categories below. Use the Words to Spark Thoughts at the end of the book to remind you of compliments those around you have made.

Personality or Character Compliments
Example: You are so nice; That was very generous of you; I really appreciate how welcoming you have been; You are a great friend

Training/Knowledge-Based/Learned Compliments
Example: Shannon is the expert in our group; If you need help with that issue, Bob is the person to call; You are such a great driver; Can you show me how to use this software

Soft Skills Compliments
Example: You are a great networker; You are a real self-starter; Creativity just comes naturally to you; I enjoy hearing you speak

Are there strengths for which you rarely receive compliments? How can you better showcase or communicate these strengths through your strategic job responsibilities in order to receive compliments?

Example: Editing skills are not complimented. Will start sending manager redline version instead of only clean version to show all my edits.

well. We'll talk more about how to collect and communicate your accomplishments in Chapters 10 and 11.

> **SUCCESS STRATEGY: Generating compliments and other feedback**
>
> If you don't feel like you receive compliments or feedback, you need to find a way to generate some. Often this takes time and requires a shift in your workplace environment. Some workplaces just don't seem to foster compliments or feedback. But you can change that by trying these:
>
> - Give compliments to others
> - Solicit feedback when an event occurs (discussed later in this chapter)
> - Use online survey tools to solicit anonymous feedback, which might make people feel more comfortable in the beginning
> - Ask specific open-ended questions, not yes/no questions
> - Recognize that most people are not comfortable giving feedback
> - Accept feedback, whether positive or negative, with appreciation and try to implement a response; more feedback will follow if people think you really want it

Weaknesses

On the flip side of the coin are the negatives or weaknesses we all possess. Again, a dreaded and common interview question is "What are your weaknesses?" What do you struggle with? What is an area you feel needs improvement? Just like with strengths, you may have weaknesses in a variety of areas. Weaknesses, large and small, must be considered. Remember, you don't have to hate your weaknesses. A weakness can easily be something you enjoy or want to do better – people who excel are typically not satisfied with their current state and are striving to do better. Considering the same categories we used for strengths and compliments, use **Action Box 25** to explore your weaknesses.

Many people find training, knowledge-based, or learned weaknesses relatively easy to identify because we generally know

ACTION BOX 25: List Your Weaknesses

List your weaknesses in each of the three categories. Use the Words to Spark Thoughts at the end of the book if needed.

Personality or Character Weaknesses
Example: Harsh; Impatient; Rude; Overbearing; Perpetually late

Training/Knowledge-Based/Learned Weaknesses
Example: Run too slow; Need to improve software skills; Not accurate at target shooting

Soft Skills Weaknesses
Example: Managing people; Communication techniques; Negotiating; Managing meetings

where we need improvement technically. However, weaknesses in personality or soft skills may be more difficult as they are subjective and not easily defined. If you have completed a personality assessment or seminar, you may be able to pull relevant information on your soft skills weaknesses. You should also refer to your last performance review and note the weaknesses your manager identified.

Weaknesses do not need to be limiting factors in your career. We all have them. And we all have different weaknesses. You must understand what yours are so that they are not highlighted in your performance on a regular basis. Knowing your weaknesses allows you to surround yourself with others who compliment you. This really can advance your career and allow you to capitalize on your own strengths, as well as the strengths of others.

I, Danielle, can relate to Felicia. I tend to speak before thinking when I get frustrated or am passionate about an issue. Generally

Felicia had recently graduated from college and was taking every opportunity to participate in potential networking events in her new community. She attended an alumni program sponsored by her university one evening where she received what she considered the best advice she'd ever heard about her weaknesses. Felicia was told that her weaknesses would always be the same weaknesses throughout her career.

Weaknesses are sometimes habits, but generally they are related to our personality or innate skills. Felicia taught herself to capitalize on her weaknesses or surround herself with people who complemented her weaknesses. This advice has taken Felicia significantly further in her career than trying to cover up or change who she is.

Know yourself and use others' skills to compensate for your weaknesses.

this happens at a bad time and can cause problems for me or those around me. I have developed relationships with coworkers who know that I have this weakness. Thankfully, they can see it coming and stop me before I say too much. As much as I try, I still tend to stick my foot in my mouth at times, but not as much as I would if my coworkers weren't there to save me.

Does achieving the top rating on your performance review depend on your thriving within one of your weakness areas? If only one or two weaknesses need to be turned into strengths, remember that sometimes you do get an "A" for effort. Showing your manager how you address your weaknesses and work toward turning them into strengths can lead to a positive performance review. You may not have to change something about yourself; you can simply find the resources within your organization to help you succeed.

Use **Action Box 26** to define any weaknesses that you feel are holding you back from succeeding in your current position.

If your job expectations encompass many of your weaknesses, you may be in a difficult position and it may be worth exploring options that allow you to focus on your strengths. The quicker we recognize disconnects and find our way back to the right path, the better we feel and the easier it is to showcase how we *Exceed Expectations.*

Comments

Just like compliments can validate our strengths, comments can validate our weaknesses. Comments are those words that perhaps sting a bit or make you pause to consider how you could have done something differently. What do you hear from those around you? In your past performance reviews, what areas of improvement have been noted? These types of comments are often made in a light-hearted joking matter, but there is generally some truth

---

ACTION BOX 26: Address Your Weaknesses

Which weaknesses are limiting you from *Exceeding Expectations* on your performance review? What can you do to improve these weaknesses or to address them during your performance review?

Example: Punctuality is a problem, need to discuss morning child drop-off situation with my manager and alter my work hours if possible.

---

in teasing. Using the same categories as used to identify strengths, compliments and weaknesses, use **Action Box 27** to write down the comments you've received.

Perception is reality. If others have formed a perception of you or the work you do, then you are challenged to change this perception and to communicate your own personal brand. Do the comments you recorded in Action Box 27 show up regularly in your performance review or in conversations with your manager? If your manager is hearing or making these types of comments, it may be time to consider how to address them. What steps can you take to show progress is being made in a problem area? If you feel the comment is unwarranted, document and share your successes in such a way as to counter the negative comments. Showcase the positives and the contributions you are making. Changing perceptions is up to you and depends greatly on your ability to communicate your positive spin effectively.

ACTION BOX 27: Record Comments

List the comments you hear from others in each of the categories. If you need some ideas, use the Words to Spark Thoughts at the end of the book.

What comments do you hear?

Personality or Character Comments
Example: With friends like you, who needs enemies; Lighten up, everyone is doing their best; No need to insult everyone else on the team

Training/Knowledge-Based/Learned Comments
Example: Have you thought about taking a class in that area; Let's meet tomorrow so you better understand the issues; Do you need some assistance

Soft Skills Comments
Example: Wow, nobody wants to be on your team; I don't understand what you mean; You really gave that product away

Samantha has always maintained separate work and social friendships and guarded her work persona to maintain a very professional reputation. However, with her friends she is the life of the party. Few of Samantha's friends knew she was a Vice President at a major corporation.

Recently, Samantha was at a friend's birthday party and made a new contact with someone who had a similar business interest. When Samantha handed her business card to this new contact, he read her title out loud just as the birthday girl walked up. Imagine Samantha's surprise and embarrassment when her close friend heard her professional title and said "I had no idea you were smart!" That was the biggest eye-opener Samantha had in a long time. Her social network image was not a successful businesswoman. She had no idea that her social persona was overshadowing her intelligence and business success among her friends.

Understand that others' perceptions of you can cross social and professional networks.

Seeking Feedback

Make sure you give others compliments and feedback to help create an environment that encourages feedback. If you feel like you don't get feedback on a regular basis, it is your responsibility to solicit it. Ask for it! Many people are uncomfortable asking for feedback, but here are some simple ways to ask for feedback in a variety of workplace situations.

These examples provide you with a framework that can be applied to any situation in the workforce. Some subjects are much more difficult to approach. Just practice saying it before you use it at work. Practice with a friend, spouse or trusted coworker. Practice in front of the mirror. Practice on your drive to work. The more you say something out loud, the more comfortable you'll be using

Soliciting Feedback

Situation	Sample Question
Presentation	I felt like people struggled with the financial slides in my presentation today. What could I have done to make the data easier to understand?
Meeting	I wasn't getting much feedback in the meeting today. Were the ideas I presented clear? What could have made it more attractive?
Document Review	I presented the information in a new format to make the numbers clearer. Was it easier to understand our proposal?
Attire	I'm struggling with our dress code that encourages 'smart' attire. You always look very professional. Do you have any tips on how to enhance my wardrobe to appear smarter?
Communication	Jim doesn't seem to value the ideas I share in our team meetings. Do you have any thoughts on how I can communicate my ideas more effectively?
Networking	You seem to know everyone in our industry. Do you have tips on how I can start building my own network?

it when needed. And we all need to ask for feedback at work. If we don't ask for it, we may never get it!

Once you've received feedback, you must respond positively. Sometimes you will consider the feedback to be valuable and sometimes you will think the person is crazy. However, remember the important part of this interaction is to understand what others perceive to be true. If you react by saying "You're crazy," that person will never give you feedback again. Likely, others will hear of your reaction and they will not give you feedback either. Be appreciative, be polite, be professional and really think about what you have been told. Some easy ways to respond are as follows:

- That's a great idea.
- I never thought of that angle.
- I really appreciate your honesty.
- I appreciate your expertise in this area.
- I always learn something from talking with you.

Even if you don't agree with the feedback, acknowledge it and thank the person for sharing with you.

Examining our strengths and weaknesses and paying attention to the compliments and comments we receive give us insights into our true selves. Can you draw connections across the four exercises and tie them to your job expectations and your performance review metrics? What trends do you see in the notes you've made about yourself? Perhaps you have a list reflective of your outgoing personality, your desire to spend time with others or your desire to spend reflective time by yourself. You may discover that you *Exceed Expectations* on your performance review in all areas you listed as strengths, but, your overall rating is being pulled down by areas tied to your weaknesses.

These connections and the links to your goals and those of your manager and your organization should guide your performance review communications. They should also highlight areas you need to either focus on or emphasize more as you move toward *Exceeding Expectations*. Making these links will help you better understand yourself and better express yourself in your upcoming performance review. As we move forward, we'll use this data to tie everything together, along with the goals you will develop in Chapter 9.

Chapter 8 Takeaways

Reveal the Real You

- You must know who you are before you can determine where you are headed.

- Determine what you like or dislike about current and past positions to reveal your ideal work environment.

- Identify training needs by comparing work related strengths and weaknesses with your job responsibilities.

- Know yourself and use others' skills to complement your weaknesses.

- Receiving and incorporating feedback is essential to your success.

- Understand that others' perceptions of you can cross social and professional networks.

CHAPTER 9

Define Your Goals

"I will celebrate, but I know new goals and objectives will come and I am ready to take them."

Ronaldo, Brazilian Soccer Player

Strategy 2 is about correlating goals or objectives with specific job responsibilities so you can identify relevant successes in the workplace. Making the connection between your job responsibilities and the goals of you, your manager, your team, or your organization helps align your performance to various success measures. With a better understanding of yourself, you will now be ready to complete the Strategies Grid column dedicated to goals and objectives. Take a step back to think about your personal career goals and link them back to your job responsibilities through the Strategies Grid.

Reflect back on Action Boxes 22 through 27 (Strengths, Compliments, Weaknesses and Comments) that you completed in Chapter 8. Your strengths, weaknesses, compliments and comments are all a part of what you like and don't like about your current or past positions. As you develop your dream job in the next exercise, keep this information in mind as it will often highlight the intangible items we look for in a dream job. Remember that you may be great at something, but don't like doing it. There might be something that you've really enjoyed doing in a past position, but no longer feel challenged or interested in doing as you move forward.

I, Danielle, love to organize things. Early in my career I found pleasure in organizing files for myself and others, organizing events, organizing just about anything that someone asked me to. At this point in my career, I often pass those tasks along to others. Organizing events can still be fun every once in a while, but it is no longer something I want to do daily.

Dream Job

One fun and insightful technique for envisioning your future is the dream job exercise. This is something most of us have thought about, but few have ever taken the time to write down. What does

In Jason's first performance review, his supervisor asked him if he liked getting out of bed and coming to work. Jason wasn't sure how to answer this question, so he just said yes. The question really weighed on Jason's mind because the truth was that the answer was no. After months of contemplating the question, Jason realized that he hoped that when he found his dream job, it would excite him and be something he looked forward to in the morning. Jason laughed with his friends that the reason he wasn't happy at work was because he isn't a morning person. He felt lost after having devoted years to achieving his goal of becoming an engineer only to find out that it wasn't really where he thought he belonged.

Be honest about your goals – especially to yourself!

your dream job look like? Your dream job may change over time and current life influences may impact what it looks like today. By understanding what it looks like, you can have strategic conversations with your manager and align your skills development or job responsibilities to the path of your dream job. Complete the exercise in **Action Box 28** with an open mind and see what emerges.

How closely does your dream job, or the characteristics and environment of your dream job, match your current situation? Circle the dream job characteristics you've noted that are absolute MUST HAVES. This gives you a good idea of where you would like to head in the future and what to consider for future jobs. Now underline the characteristics you have in your current job. How closely aligned are you? Are there characteristics of your dream job you can incorporate into your current job responsibilities or work environment?

The dream job exercise and the comparison to your current position can be eye opening. I, Tricia, had general ideas of what I liked and didn't like early in my career, but had never taken the

ACTION BOX 28: Identify Your Dream Job

Draw it. Write it. Describe it. Use the workplace factors below to help you create a thorough picture of your dream job. Make notes under each topic about what is important to you at work. Describe what the workplace would look like for you to jump out of bed in the morning. If you are drawing a blank, use the Words to Spark Thoughts at the end of the book to get started.

Status

Example: Specific level in organization; Visibility; Title

Location

Example: A specific city; Country; At home; In a high-rise; In an industrial setting; In a retail store; Outside

Commute

Example: Never need to get into my car; Doesn't matter; By bicycle; By park-and-ride

Office Space

Example: Must have a window and a door; Cubicle is fine; My car would be great; Prefer open concept; Colors; Noise level; Don't care

ACTION BOX 28: Dream Job Continued...

Start Time

Example: Never before 10 a.m.; The earlier the better; Flexible; Middle of the day; Middle of the night

End Time

Example: Early enough to get a round of golf in before dusk; The later the better; Flexible; In time to pick up my kids from daycare

Compensation

Example: Base amount; Bonus plan; Stock; Profit sharing; Retirement contributions; Expense reimbursements; Health benefits; Dental benefits; Vision benefits; Vacation; Life insurance

Amenities

Example: Paid parking; Support professional memberships and participation; Provide continued development and training opportunities

ACTION BOX 28: Dream Job Continued...

Coworkers

Example: Prefer none; Team environment; Tight-knit group; Lots preferred; Must respect them; Must like them; Prefer a quiet group; A group that goes out for lunch every day

Culture

Example: Fun; Respectful; Competitive; Laid back; Uptight; Fast paced; Global; Local; Merit based; Tenure based; Gender makeup; Social considerations; Diversity; Management style

Attire

Example: Suits; Jeans; Uniform; Comfy shoes; Trendy; Smart; Casual; Collegiate; Classic; None required; Express yourself

Management

Example: Hands on; Autonomous; Involved; Removed; Located elsewhere

Type of Business

Example: Large corporation; Non-profit; Privately held; Family-owned; Specific industry; Size; Growth potential; Profitability

ACTION BOX 28: Dream Job Continued...

Type of Job

Example: Physical; Engages the mind; Consistent; Specific duties

Lighting

Example: Windows; Fluorescent; Sunlight; Lamps; Disco ball; Don't care

Food/Drink Options

Example: Coffee provided; Bottled water provided; Snacks available; Beer on Fridays; Lunch catered in once a month; Company shouldn't provide anything

Learning Opportunities

Example: Regular lunch-and-learns; Support conference attendance; Support research and presenting at conferences; Soft-skills training; Technical training

Responsibilities

Example: Bring it on; Want to walk away at the end of the day; Want to manage employees; Want to manage projects; Want to manage research; Want to manage volunteers

ACTION BOX 28: Dream Job Continued...

Travel

Example: None; Some; 50%; 75%; 100%; Domestic; International; Never at home; Short trips; Long trips

Amount of Change

Example: Like stability; Hate stability; Like my days to be consistent; Want to do something new every few months; Need to be able to plan ahead; Energized by new challenges

Growth Opportunities

Example: Opportunity to learn; Take on management roles; Set career paths; Prefer no growth

Social Issues

Example: Community involvement; Charity involvement; Green issues; Cultural issues; Generational considerations

Other Characteristics

Example: Art on the walls; Quality of furniture; Body art respected; Music played on the loud speaker; Hip and trendy; Acceptance of alternative lifestyles...what else is important to you?

time to imagine this dream job where everything would be perfect in my career. After walking through this exercise and drawing a picture of my dream job, I was amazed at the power of the picture I had drawn. The picture looked nothing like my current state. It was eye opening to put down on paper how different my vision of the future was. After the exercise, I began to develop the skills and networks needed to move me closer to my dream job. It opened me to a wider realm of possibilities that I had never considered before. I was very thankful to have done the exercise early in my career. I am now midcareer and in my dream job and career in education. It is easier for me to *Exceed Expectations* on my performance review because I truly love where I am and the work I am doing. It's easy to shine when your passions align with your organization's mission. I may have another dream career after this one, but having that first picture of that perfect job has continued to guide my skills development, communications and career decisions.

Keep in mind your dream job can change over time. When I, Danielle, started my career, my dream job incorporated suits, a fancy office, an ideal job title and all the perks that come with corporate life. As I achieved many of these items, they became less attractive than I thought they would be. Now I'd prefer a commercial flight over the stress of a corporate jet any day. Twenty years ago I never would have believed elements of my dream job would change so dramatically.

Now that you've defined your dream job, it's time to develop a plan to get it. Your performance review and your communications with your manager can help you get closer to that dream job. Use your performance review to share your dreams and goals, and to align your conversation to the organization's structure or goals. Completing the Strategies Grid will give you some tools to help accomplish this.

Your Goals

Setting goals is the best way to take small steps toward the larger, more futuristic goal of that dream job. Goals must be defined and measurable. They should be **SMART**: Specific, Measurable, Achievable, Realistic, and Timely. The more detail your goals have, the more likely you are to reach for them and attain them. Writing goals defines them and makes them real. Goals provide direction and motivation and are useful in communicating to your manager in a performance review where you want to go and how you want to get there.

- **S**pecific: The goal must answer the 5 W's – who, what, when, where and why. You should be able to see, touch, smell, taste or hear the results of the goal.

- **M**easurable: You should know if the goal has been achieved or how you are progressing toward the goal. There should be milestones you can track.

- **A**chievable: The goal should be attainable. It must be possible. Otherwise, why would you even want to try?

- **R**ealistic: The goal should be something you are capable of and interested in achieving. Unrealistic goals would not be worth pursuing.

- **T**imely: The goal should include a timeframe. When will you complete the task?

Goals should cover all areas of one's life and can generally be divided into three categories: 1) professional, 2) educational and 3) personal or family. Even though we're focused on the workplace and your professional space, the other goal categories may impact your motivations, opportunities and other priorities related to your performance review. For you, each category may include several goals; however, too many can lead to a lack of focus or may simply become overwhelming. Goals can be far-reaching – those goals you want to achieve by the end of your lifetime. Goals can also be short-term, such as one-year or five-year goals. Short-term goals help define intermediate steps on your way to your lifetime goals.

Your dream job is the easiest way we have found to approach goal-setting. Your dream job feeds directly into your lifetime goals which break into your five and then one-year goals. Once you progress down to your one-year goals, it is easier to map them to your strategic job responsibilities and tie them to your organizational goals in the Strategies Grid.

Goal-setting can be broken down into eight basic steps. First, you need to define what you want or need; define what you want to accomplish or have. Break it into smaller pieces, smaller steps that are more easily actionable. Write it all down so it becomes real and you become more accountable. Make it SMART. Review the goal periodically to remind yourself of where you are headed. Check your progress and mark any milestones along the way. Revise the goal as needed, as your values or priorities change, as your organization or environment changes. Finally, celebrate the goal once you have achieved it and be sure others know you have accomplished it.

SUCCESS STRATEGY: 8 Steps to Goal Setting

1. Want it or need it
2. Break it into pieces
3. Write it down
4. Make it SMART
5. Review it
6. Check progress and mark milestones
7. Revise it
8. Celebrate it

Lifetime Goals

By the end of your lifetime, what do you want to have accomplished in your career? Is your dream job the job from which you plan to retire, or do you have ambitions beyond it? Defining your lifetime career goals ensures you stay focused throughout your career and should guide your communications and performance reviews.

Lifetime goals often lack some of the SMART characteristics; the timeframes, for example, may be less defined. Don't get bogged down in providing lots of details if you don't have them. The aim of defining your lifetime goals is to help you provide some direction for your short-term goals. Don't forget to define your lifetime goals for each category – professional, educational and personal or family. Each can affect your motivations. It is important to see the complete picture of where you want to be in the future. Use **Action Box 29** to write down your lifetime goals.

As an example, consider setting lifetime goals based upon a dream job of owning your own business. Your lifetime goals might look like the following:

- *Professional*: Own my own business within the next 15 years. My business will help others to achieve their personal and professional goals.

- *Educational*: Engage in continued learning and advancement of knowledge through continuing education, books, online tools or other learning means.

- *Personal or Family*: Have a home of my own and a loving, supportive and engaged family.

ACTION BOX 29: Define Your Lifetime Goals

Write down your lifetime goals for each of the categories listed or for other areas that make sense to you.

Examples are provided on page 138.

Professional Lifetime Goals:

Educational Lifetime Goals:

Personal or Family Lifetime Goals:

Five-Year Goals

Five-year goals bring your lifetime goals a bit closer to reality. Five-year goals should be SMART; they should be much more defined and more clearly actionable than your lifetime goals. As the timeframe of a goal becomes closer, it should be more tangible and measurable. I, Danielle, have a lifetime goal of having a home that serves as a personal retreat for me and my family. Over the years, my five-year goals have included things such as purchase adjoining property to have space to install a pool, remove all carpet in the house and install wood floors, and replace all windows in the house to create a quieter and more energy efficient environment. The five-year goals create a 'to do' list for me while the lifetime goal creates a vision of what I want my home to be in the future.

If five years does not work for you, it is your plan, choose three years or ten years or some intermediate length of time that makes sense for you and your lifetime goals.

Use **Action Box 30** to break your lifetime goals into shorter, SMARTer five-year goals.

Envision what you can accomplish as an intermediate step to achieving your lifetime goal. Your five-year goals help you move past what you can accomplish in the near future and give you time to adjust your career path, to develop skills, or to make other modifications that may take time to achieve. Continuing with the example of the dream job of owning your own business, five-year goals might look like the following:

- *Professional*: Develop a business plan for my own business.

- *Educational*: Complete an MBA degree with an emphasis on finance and accounting.

- *Personal or Family*: Start a family.

I, Tricia, struggle with five-year goals. I have things I want to accomplish in my lifetime and I have things I want to accomplish

ACTION BOX 30: Define Your Five-Year Goals

Write down your five-year goals for each of the categories listed or for other areas that make sense to you.

Examples are provided on page 140.

Professional Five-Year Goals:

Educational Five-Year Goals:

Personal or Family Five-Year Goals:

this year, but my intermediate goals are not defined in a time-frame. I understand what I like and where my strengths lie so I keep those in mind as I look to the future. Five-year goals are meant to bridge the gap from short-term to lifetime goals. Even though I don't specifically define five-year goals, I know what I hope to accomplish somewhere between now and the end of my lifetime. Writing five-year goals works for many people and ensures progress is being made toward lifetime career goals. You determine what works best to keep you moving forward. What works for me is keeping my vision of the future clearly in front of me. Every year I define my next steps and pay close attention to the one-year goals I set.

One-Year Goals and Milestones

Once you've developed your five-year goals, break them down further to one-year goals. One-year goals should also be SMART. They should take you one small step closer to your lifetime goals, align with your five-year goals and set you on the path you desire.

Your one-year goals should also incorporate the goals for your job responsibilities. The goals for your job responsibilities may be driven by your manager or organization, but it is important to include them and keep sight of them as you prepare for your performance review. Not all of your personal goals will end up on your Strategies Grid or in your performance review. However, if you are able to strategically include personal goals and map them to your strategic job responsibilities, your manager will be aware of your ambitions. It will open the door to strategic communications that will move you closer to your dream job.

Be careful not to go overboard or overly commit yourself. Realistically think about what you can accomplish in the next year. Consider the other commitments you have in your life. If you have a huge project at work, are training for a marathon and

Fran was a young accountant whose personal situation had moved her to rural Oklahoma. She was quickly moving up the ladder in her company and her personal reason for being in Oklahoma had changed. She really wanted to move to Chicago, corporate headquarters. This became a five-year goal for Fran. Every year in her performance review, she made sure her manager knew she would welcome a move to Chicago. She always wrote it on the comments section of her review form "Willing to relocate – would welcome position in Chicago."

One Thursday morning as she was getting out of her car, she noticed a senior manager arriving at the same time. She slowed her pace to take the opportunity to talk with him. He casually mentioned that he was having trouble filling a position in Chicago – did Fran know anyone who'd be interested? Fran was ready and immediately expressed her interest. Her next stop was to talk to her manager about this parking lot conversation. On Friday, Fran was asked to be in Chicago for an interview Monday and Tuesday. On Monday, they asked her to take Wednesday to look at housing options. On Thursday she was offered the position and on Friday she accepted the new job. She reported to work in Chicago less than 2 weeks from that parking lot conversation.

Have goals and look for opportunities to achieve them.

just got engaged, adding 30 one-year goals to the mix may just send you over the edge. However, if you know that these things are a part of the next year, incorporate into your one-year goals what needs to be accomplished for the things you've already committed to. Throughout your career and your life, you will be forced to prioritize your goals, activities, and aspirations.

Use **Action Box 31** to break your goals down further, into SMARTer, short-term one-year goals. Be sure to include the goals related to your job responsibilities. You will likely have a lot more one-year goals than lifetime or five-year goals.

ACTION BOX 31: Define Your One-Year Goals

Write down your one-year goals for each of the categories listed or for other areas that make sense to you.

Examples are provided on page 145.

Professional One-Year Goals:

Educational One-Year Goals:

Personal or Family One-Year Goals:

For the example of the dream job of owning your own business, one-year goals might look like the following:

- *Professional*: Position myself at my current company in a job where I can learn management practices, accounting and human resources.

- *Educational*: Apply to graduate school.

- *Personal or Family*: Purchase a home.

One-year goals can be broken down even further to milestones throughout the year. Milestones provide checkpoints to help you continue to progress toward your goals. They also allow for celebrations along the way.

In the example of the dream job of owning your own business, some milestones might look like:

- *Professional*: Update my resume within the next month. Determine which positions at my current company would offer management skills within three months.

- *Educational*: Identify graduate schools by June. Take GMAT in October. Get applications for graduate schools by December.

- *Personal or Family*: Identify a realtor within the next two months. Identify budget for purchase no later than Halloween. Pre-qualify for home mortgage loan within one month of determining budget.

I, Danielle, have always been a goal setter and when I was in high school, I developed goals that all began with "by the time I am 30." I was focused and achieved each of these goals. Then I was lost. I had been focused on the same goals for so long that I never stopped to create new milestones or a new vision for my future. I spent a year with no real direction. When I finally took the time to set new goals and a new direction for myself, I was revived.

Frank was very goal-oriented, and had been since he was a small child. When he was young he set goals that he strived to reach by the time he turned 30 years old. At 28, Frank realized he had accomplished all but one – a salary metric that he had set for himself. Once he put his mind to it, Frank easily reached that goal. Then the big challenge arose.

Frank was focused on the same set of goals for such a long time that, once he had accomplished them, he was lost. That is when he decided to take some advice a friend had given him – give yourself a day every year to revisit existing goals and develop new ones. Frank finds that this will ultimately get him where he'd like to be. He knows the power of what can be accomplished if you focus on it. Frank is now focused on accomplishing all those evolving things that he randomly says he will do someday. Goal setting is the most important thing Frank does for himself all year.

Small steps lead to achievements – set goals and go for it.

Goal-setting can be difficult for all of us, even natural goal-setters like me. However, once you've invested the time in yourself to set a direction, a vision, a goal, a dream – whatever you want to call it – things just seem to fall into place.

Connect to the Strategies Grid

Once you understand your one-year goals, it is time to connect them to your job responsibilities in the Strategies Grid. While not all of your personal one-year goals will make it into the Strategies Grid, it is important to incorporate them where possible as a means to communicate to your manager. For the dream job example of owning your own business, consider how to incorporate your personal one-year goal of positioning yourself at your current company where you can learn management practices, accounting and human resources. If your current strategic job responsibilities do not include accounting but are tied to a project with a budget, you could include a goal to learn the budgeting process for your project. You could also, through strategic communications with your manager, position yourself to include a goal of assuming responsibility for the project budget or some aspect of the accounting process during the next year. By understanding your dream job and how that translates down to one-year goals, you can begin to align your current experiences and job responsibilities. You can begin to take control of your performance review and career plan. Use **Action Box 32** to connect your job responsibilities to your personal goals or objectives.

As we move forward, the objective is to build your final Strategies Grid. It is unlikely that your final Strategies Grid will look like the tidy chart provided as an example in Chapter 1. Instead, you will likely have multiple goals or objectives listed for each job responsibility. Your Strategies Grid must work for you – use multiple table cells or bullets for each job responsibility's goals and objectives to help make it easier.

Sitting down once a year to prepare for a performance review will help you achieve high performance ratings, but it won't move you forward. You must integrate tools such as understanding yourself and goal-setting to take this next step. Understanding your goals and how they align with your manager's and organization's goals, values and priorities can help you *Exceed Expectations* on your performance review. It can also put into perspective what *Exceeds Expectations* means to you, which areas of your job are most important to you, and the path to your lifetime goals.

Aligning job responsibilities with your personal goals as the Strategies Grid demonstrates will propel your career forward and help you achieve your definition of success. However, the performance evaluation process is specifically about how successful you are in your current job. Your boss is likely to be more concerned with your meeting specific job goals rather than personal career

ACTION BOX 32: Connect Personal Goals to Job Responsibilities

Make the connections to the Strategies Grid and your performance review process. What existing goals or objectives do you have for each job responsibility? What can you do to incorporate your personal one-year goals into the goals or objectives for your job responsibilities?

Strategy 1	Strategy 2
Job Responsibilities	Goals or Objectives
Example: Prepare and submit accurate monthly revenue report to management team	*Example: Work Goal – accurate and timely information; Personal Goal – learn financial aspects of business to later apply to running my own company*

goals. Job goals should be SMART, just like personal goals. Job goals should include specific metrics that you and your manager have agreed upon well before the performance review happens. Each job responsibility can have multiple goals. Some will only be aligned with a job goal while others will be aligned with both a job goal, and a personal goal. Your objective is to ensure that you know which specific goal equates to success for your manager for each of your job responsibilities.

Align SMART Goals to Job Responsibilities

Job Responsibilities	Goals
Manage operations of a $3 million division within budget and in accordance with organizational goals.	Meet revenue goal of $3 million and operating budget of $1.3 million for fiscal year. Meet organizational goals of 85% employee retention and 75% excellent ratings on customer service this fiscal year.
Develop 30 strategic partnerships to expand market share.	Develop 15 strategic partnerships with existing customers and 15 with new customers this fiscal year. Expand market share by 5% this fiscal year.
Advance the organization's reputation and technology leadership by participating in and presenting at 6 national conferences and events.	Present information on new products at 2 national conferences in 2011. Moderate technical panel at 2 regional conferences in 2011. Host 2 events for our customers and employees to share new technologies in 2011.
Be identified as a technology expert while providing technical assistance to over 75 customers.	Attend 2 training classes to advance technical knowledge before the end of the fiscal year. Implement customer survey system to demonstrate that group is providing technical assistance to customers before June 2011.
Other strategic duties as assigned that contribute to the organization's mission and goals.	Organize file system so that documents can be found in less than 10 minutes by October 2010. Implement training program for new hires on general office policies before next summer internship class starts. Reduce office supply budget by 30% in next fiscal year.

Use **Action Box 33** to identify the goals you and your manager have defined for each of your job responsibilities.

As you did when you connected personal goals to job responsibilities in Action Box 32, the objective is to build your final Strategies Grid. Again, you will likely have multiple goals or objectives listed for each job responsibility. Use multiple table cells or bullets for each job responsibility's goals and objectives to help make it easier.

Chapter 9 Takeaways

Define Your Goals

- Goal setting is critical to long-term success.

- Agreeing on SMART goals with your manager leads to performance review success.

- Be honest about your goals – especially to yourself!

- Have goals and look for opportunities to achieve them.

- Personal goals should be integrated into professional goals.

- Your dream job helps define your lifetime, five-year, and one-year goals.

- Small steps lead to achievements – set goals and go for it.

ACTION BOX 33: Connect Job Specific Goals to Job Responsibilities

Make the connections to the Strategies Grid and your performance review process. What existing goals or objectives do you have for each job responsibility? How can you align these with your manager's and/or organization's goals?

Strategy 1	Strategy 2
Job Responsibilities	Goals or Objectives
Example: Prepare and submit accurate monthly revenue report to management team	*Example: Work Goal – accurate and timely information; Manager Goal – presented in attractive format that highlights successes; Organization Goal – submit timely reports to shareholders which include this data*

Collect and Communicate Accomplishments

Strategies Grid

Strategy 1	Strategy 2	Strategy 3	Strategy 4	Strategy 5
Job Responsibilities	Goals or Objectives	Accomplishments	Challenges	Success Methods

By now you should have a deeper understanding of your job, your environment and yourself. With this understanding, you can begin to impact perceptions and ultimately impact your performance review. You will *Exceed Expectations* on your performance review if you communicate strategically and effectively about the positive impact you have on your organization and the visible value you create. The remaining strategies begin to take this understanding and move you toward concrete actions that can positively affect your performance review. Strategy 3 focuses on accomplishments – collecting them for your job responsibilities and effectively communicating them to your manager and others who influence your performance review.

CHAPTER 10

Collect Your Accomplishments

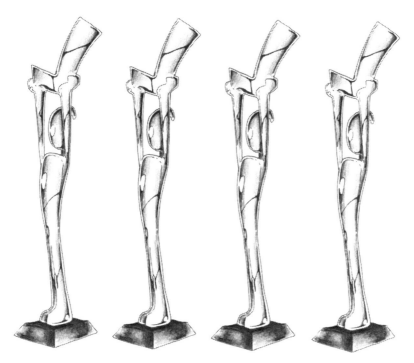

"It had long since come to my attention that people of accomplishment rarely sit back and let things happen to them. They went out and happened to things."

Leonardo da Vinci, Famous Artist and Scientist

Can you remember what you accomplished earlier today? What about yesterday? How about ten months ago? It is very difficult to recall what has been accomplished over the past year without reminders. In the moment, it is hard to believe we can forget such a stellar accomplishment. Unfortunately, we often forget the most important ones when we are pressed to list our accomplishments for a performance review or job interview or award application. By creating a system for collecting your accomplishments, they are there when you need to share them or compile them for your review. They become easily accessible and easy to recall.

Performance Review Usage – Define Your Needs

Consider how you will use your accomplishments before deciding which system is best for you. How will you best collect and organize your accomplishments? To better understand your needs, consider the following questions:

- Do you need to easily recall accomplishments for an annual performance review – a once a year event?

- Do you need to create monthly or regular accomplishment updates for your team, manager or organization?

- Do you report your goal status at a regular staff or project meeting?

- Do you need concrete examples of your accomplishments for your career development plan, performance review or one-on-ones with your manager?

- Do you need to be reminded of how valuable you are when you are having a frustrating or bad day at work?

- Are you anticipating a job change, career shift or a life change that will be enhanced by documented results?

- Are you considering starting your own business and need marketing material accomplishment points?

Accomplishments don't just happen at work. Your personal, volunteer and educational accomplishments can also have an impact on your work and your performance review. Completing a degree program is a large accomplishment that may not have been financially supported by your employer, but will now support a raise or promotion. Managing a team of 30 volunteers in a non-profit organization will certainly hone your abilities to manage a larger group of employees at the office. Completing a marathon demonstrates your ability to aim high and work toward a long-term goal. Making a presentation to your child's class about the work you do gives the company valuable marketing exposure because every child may tell their parents about your presentation or the teacher may share throughout his or her network.

Keeping up with **all** your accomplishments, big and small, can be a challenge with all your daily demands. Once you have defined your needs, it is easier to understand how to collect and organize your accomplishments. Three easy ways to collect your accomplishments include: 1) the accomplishments reservoir; 2) kind words and compliments bin; and 3) curriculum vitae. These are all valuable when you need to recall the details about your accomplishments. A fourth place to collect high-level, less detailed information is your resume. Your resume can serve as a great communication tool to showcase your accomplishment highlights. Of course, each of these tools can be tailored for how you will use them. You may use all of them or some combination of them, maybe storing different information in different places. The key is to collect all of your accomplishments in a way that makes sense for you. Then, when you need it for your performance review, you will have the information readily available.

Accomplishments Reservoir

Your accomplishments reservoir is the quickest and easiest way to collect your accomplishments throughout the year. This can be a list, a file folder, a basket, a drawer, an email folder, any mechanism to hold your accomplishments in one place. Each time you achieve a goal, receive an award or collect some sort of accomplishment, deposit it into your accomplishments reservoir so you can easily find it for your performance review or other needs, such as a job interview or award application. Don't discount an accomplishment as being too small – it could be the basis for something much larger in the future. At the same time, don't forget to include the really big accomplishments. We often think we'll never forget the moment, and then months of busy days and bigger accomplishments later, we can no longer remember the details.

> Clara keeps a training folder in which she places those free business pertinent topic webinars and phone presentations that she attends in her lunch or other free time. She uses these to evidence how she stays current in knowledge related to her job and those areas that she doesn't have a formal education in. She can then use that knowledge in speaking with business associates to bolster trust and confidence in her abilities.
>
> **The accomplishments reservoir can and should include anything that can enhance your career.**

Organization of your accomplishments reservoir depends on your planned use of the collection. Create a file system that works best for you and your needs. Consider how you will handle hand-written notes, emails, verbal acknowledgements, and more formal review results. You may need to have both an electronic and a physical accomplishments reservoir. If the reservoir is used to update a resume, then a chronological collection may be most useful. If the reservoir is used to prepare for a performance review, then a goal-based collection might be the most useful. One, or more likely a combination of options, should work for you.

Accomplishments Reservoir Organization Options

Option	Put Into Action
Chronological	Place accomplishments in your file system in order by date. You may have one folder for each month of the year and sort accomplishments on a monthly basis. You may need just one file for your electronic accomplishments reservoir as electronic records are easy to sort by date.
Goal or Objective	Place accomplishments in your file system by goals or objectives, either organizational or personal/professional. It may be useful to have one folder for each goal with associated accomplishments filed in chronological order.
Job Function	Place accomplishments in your file system according to the various job functions for which you may be evaluated. It may be useful to have one folder for each job function with associated accomplishments filed chronologically.
Business Area	Place accomplishments in your file system according to the various business areas in which you may be evaluated. It may be useful to have one folder for each with associated accomplishments filed in chronological order.
Category	Place accomplishments in your file system according to various evaluated categories such as awards, customer reviews, work recognitions, task completion, etc. It may be useful to have one folder for each category you define with associated accomplishments in chronological order.
Ad Hoc	Perhaps the easiest and probably the most common initial option is placing accomplishments in one electronic and/or one physical file without worrying about order. This gets you in the habit of collecting the materials to make them available to you, though you may not easily find what you need when you need it.

Your accomplishments reservoir should be updated on a regular basis for it to be effective and useful. At a minimum, take fifteen minutes once a month to brainstorm, collect or file accomplishments. Ideally, as soon as you have an accomplishment, you file it in the appropriate place and your file stays updated. In addition, be sure you capture the details of the accomplishment such as the date, project referenced, solution or award criteria, and any key results so you can recall them when needed.

I, Danielle, have never moved past the ad hoc collection system. It continues to work for me and provides an easy way to collect accomplishments that are available when I need them. Use **Action Box 34** to plan how you will set up your accomplishments reservoir. The more detail you can provide, the easier it will be for you to put it into action.

ACTION BOX 34: Plan Your Accomplishments Reservoir(s)

Describe how you will set up your accomplishments reservoir(s). What method(s) will you use for sorting? Where will it reside?

Example: Initial set-up as single paper file folder and single email folder. Expand into categories as necessary.

I will establish or update my accomplishments reservoir by _____ *(insert date)*.

Kind Words and Compliments Bin

You may receive short emails, note cards or other personal notes complimenting you on the work you have done, the help you provided or some other small or large accomplishment you have achieved. You may simply think, "Oh isn't that nice!" and then delete the email or toss the note in the recycling bin. But when it comes to your performance review, it is useful to have a smorgasbord of compliments to choose from. They support your efforts and show how you *Exceed Expectations*.

Having a compilation of kind words and compliments is especially important if your work serves others. Your manager may not directly receive feedback on the work you do or the services you provide to others. If the form for your performance review asks for examples, these kind words and compliments can help your manager fill in the gaps and make it easier to understand how you *Exceed Expectations*.

Just as with the accomplishments reservoir, organization of your kind words and compliments bin depends on your planned use of the collection. Establishing the same filing system as your accomplishments reservoir could be helpful. Or you may choose to combine them so everything is housed in one location. More general compliments such as those addressing your meeting management skills, conflict resolution abilities or other attributes not connected directly to one of your job functions, goals, or project areas may need their own electronic or physical file sorted in chronological order. Regardless of their format or connection to your work, all kind words and compliments, from a few words to a lengthy letter, deserve space in your accomplishments filing system.

I, Tricia, use the kind words bin extensively for myself and my team. I have a common email folder for my team where we place compliments for any of our projects and program work. To further organize the information, the common email folder has subfolders for each audience who may provide the compliments: precollege students or parents, university students, university peers or administrators, and corporate partners. I also have a kind words email bin for my work where I collect any complimentary note or word of thanks that I receive specifically for my efforts. All of these are referenced when documenting my performance or the performance of my program and team.

Use **Action Box 35** to determine how you will collect your kind words and compliments.

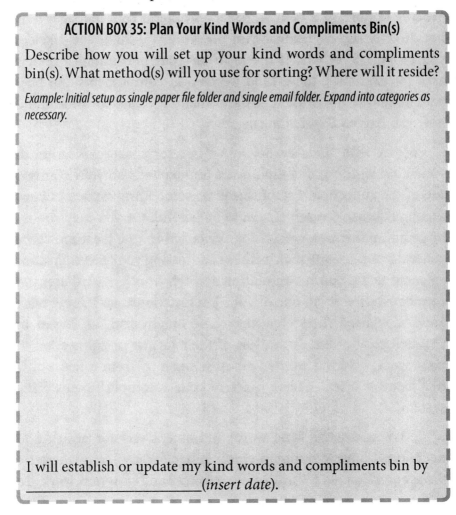

ACTION BOX 35: Plan Your Kind Words and Compliments Bin(s)

Describe how you will set up your kind words and compliments bin(s). What method(s) will you use for sorting? Where will it reside?

Example: Initial setup as single paper file folder and single email folder. Expand into categories as necessary.

I will establish or update my kind words and compliments bin by _____*(insert date)*.

Just like your accomplishments, kind words and compliments may need a reference that reminds you why you received the compliment. This can be as simple as writing on the note or card the date, event, and/or reason for the compliment. If the kind words were sent in an email, replying to the email and copying yourself with a thank you and basic details of the event will be useful for future reference. If possible, tie them to a specific job responsibility and capture the success in your Strategies Grid.

Your kind words and compliments, just like the accomplishments reservoir, should be updated on a regular basis for it to be effective and useful. Ideally, as soon as you receive a kind word or compliment, you file it in the appropriate place and your file stays updated. As with accomplishments, take at least fifteen minutes once a month to brainstorm, collect or file kind words or compliments. Save time by combining this effort with the updating of your accomplishments reservoir.

Curriculum Vitae

A curriculum vitae, or CV, is a much more detailed resume and is not limited in length. It summarizes your life history, job history, achievements and skills. While used more traditionally within the academic community or workplaces outside the United States, the CV is a useful way to collect accomplishments, job skills, experiences and more. The CV is all encompassing and may include the following categories:

- Personal/Contact Information (name, address, phone, email)

- Academic Background (degrees, majors/minors, honors, certificates)

- Professional Licenses/Certifications

- Work Experience

- Technical/Specialized Skills

- Professional/Academic Honors and Awards

- Professional Development (conferences/workshops attended, other activities)

- Research/Scholarly Activities (articles, conference proceedings, books, papers presented or published)

- Grants Acquired or Administered

- Services and Volunteer Work (academic, professional, community)

- Affiliations/Memberships

- Foreign Language Abilities/Skills

- Consulting or Presentations

- References

I, Danielle, don't really use the categories listed above. My CV is more like an expanded resume. It is simply a tool to collect my experiences, skills and accomplishments in detail. Since it is unlikely that I will ever forward the entire document to someone or use it for its intended job search purpose, I have arranged it to work for me. You should arrange your CV to work for you.

The first time you create a CV, it will take a lot of time, especially if you do not already have your resume updated and an accomplishments reservoir or compliments bins at your disposal. But once it is created, it is easy to maintain. It can be a great resource for your performance review, job interviews, award applications and other places where having your work and life history at your fingertips is useful. Since the CV contains a summary of everything job related, it should contain a synopsis of your accomplishments reservoir. It should be the one easy place to look for your most up-to-date job and experience information. When preparing for your performance review or reporting accomplishments to your manager, an updated CV should be your first stop for information to share.

I, Danielle, recently used my CV for an unexpected purpose. I was audited for continuing development classes for my Professional Engineers license. The CV included all the training classes I've attended and all the data I needed for the audit. The CV made the audit process very easy.

Your CV should be updated on a regular basis so it is relatively current or easy to update if the need arises. Your CV should be updated more frequently than your resume since it contains a running list of everything you do and all you accomplish. Use your accomplishments reservoir when updating your CV for important, relevant accomplishments to highlight or include.

Use **Action Box 36** to set a goal for yourself. What is your CV Action Plan?

ACTION BOX 36: Make Your CV Action Plan

I will begin my CV by _____ (insert date).

I will update my CV _____ (insert timeframe such as monthly, quarterly).

Did you just skip over that Action Box? I don't blame you! I, Tricia, took on the daunting task of creating a CV a few years ago. I'd already been in the workplace for well over a decade. It was a painful process to start, but once I got going, it was amazing to collect all that I had accomplished in one place. It took quite a bit of time to create it, but I have found it to be the easiest way to collect my accomplishments and work history. I have used it to apply for awards or programs and I have provided sections of it periodically to my manager so he is aware of my various publications or speaking engagements.

The first time Carl was nominated for an award, he had to collect all his accomplishments and career information. A mentor suggested he use all the information he collected to develop a CV to use for future opportunities. Carl started the process of creating a CV and, three years later, still hasn't finished it. However, Carl has now developed the habit of recording everything he accomplishes. In addition to creating a wonderful history of his personal and professional accomplishments, training, and volunteer activities, it has given him something to look at when he needs a reminder of how much he has accomplished over his career. Now Carl recommends to everyone he knows that they start a CV – no matter how long it takes to finish it.

Start your CV today by creating a file and adding to it as you have time.

Resume Update

Now that you've collected all this valuable information, you have no excuse not to keep your resume updated. A resume is a brief, one-to-two page summary of your relevant education and job experience. It is a snapshot of highlights from your CV. Brief is the key word; a resume cannot contain all of your accomplishments, all your kind words and every detail of every experience you have had throughout your career. However, a resume can provide a good overview of the most important pieces of your education and experience, and is important when entering the job market.

Resumes are typically shared when you are seeking a job but are often not shared again during your time holding that same job. However, as you move up the ranks of a company your resume may be used for proposals, advertisements and website information. A resume may not be appropriate to share during your performance review, but an updated resume may be relevant and important to share periodically with your manager. Resumes often contain your extracurricular experiences and the job-related skills you have gained. These are two performance indicators your manager may or may not realize. This high-level, brief summary of your experiences and skills can remind your manager why you were hired for the job in the first place. The resume can also highlight areas where you *Exceed Expectations* in a format unique from the traditional performance review or status update.

Your resume should be updated on a regular basis so it is relatively current or easy to update when the need arises. You never know when your dream job may become available. I, Tricia, learned of a fantastic opportunity and was asked to send a resume. Luckily, I had recently updated my resume and only needed to re-arrange a couple of items to highlight some particular strengths. I was able to send my resume that afternoon, had an interview scheduled within a day and had the job two weeks later. Ever since that opportunity, I have kept my resume current and ready for whatever may be around the next corner. Remember that luck is when opportunity meets preparedness.

Choose a regular interval, such as monthly, quarterly or every six months, and set a reminder so you don't forget. Since the resume contains less detail than the other accomplishments storage areas, reviewing less frequently may be appropriate. Remember to review your accomplishments reservoir and CV when updating your resume for important, relevant accomplishments to highlight or include. Use **Action Box 37** to set an interval goal for yourself to update your resume.

ACTION BOX 37: Make Your Resume Action Plan

I will update my resume every _____ *(insert timeframe such as monthly, quarterly, year).*

Collecting Your Accomplishments Tools

Tool	When to Use	How Often to Update
Accomplishments Reservoir	Performance Review, Promotion Opportunities, Award Submissions, Job Applications, Resume Updates	Minimally monthly so accomplishments aren't forgotten
Kind Words and Compliments Bin	Mental Lift, Performance Review, Award Submissions, Resume Updates	As receive them to simply collect rather than delete or forget them
Curriculum Vitae (CV)	Award Submissions, Resume Tuning for a Specific Job, Internal Corporate Marketing, Personal Marketing Efforts	Monthly, or as needed, drop items in as they occur
Resume	Job Search, Award Applications, Internal Corporate Marketing, Personal Marketing Efforts	Ideally quarterly, minimally annually

Chapter 10 Takeaways

Collect Your Accomplishments

- The accomplishments reservoir can and should include anything that can enhance your career.

- Develop a method to easily collect your workplace, volunteer, and personal accomplishments.

- Find a way to capture verbal, email and other forms of compliments.

- Even the most stellar accomplishments can be forgotten over time. Capturing them on paper reminds you of the details at performance review time.

- Start your CV today by creating a file and adding to it as you have time.

CHAPTER 11

Communicate Your Accomplishments

"You get whatever accomplishment you are willing to declare."

Georgia O'Keeffe, Famous American Artist

When corporations launch a product, the message is not left to chance. It is calculated, targeted and delivered with intention. So, why do we leave promotion of ourselves in the hands of others? Once you understand who you are, make sure you communicate your real self strategically with others. It is up to you to market yourself to your manager and others within and outside your organization. Unless you happen to have your own agent like a movie star or famous athlete, it's up to you to spread the word on how fabulous you are and how you provide value to the organization. You need to market your technical skills and abilities. Get the message out there so you can *Exceed Expectations* at every step along the way.

Ensure that your marketing efforts and message accurately reflect the product you are selling. Let your peers, friends, family, managers, employees, EVERYONE know where you want to be and what you are accomplishing throughout the process. Be strategic in both who you market yourself to (your target audience) and how. In this chapter, we'll explore five personal marketing strategies:

1. Identify your target audience

2. Define your brand and promote it

3. Create visible value

4. Seek opportunities to shine

5. Share and celebrate your accomplishments

A sixth strategy for marketing yourself, communicate strategically, was described in Chapter 1.

Identify Your Target Audience

When sharing performance related communications, from celebrating accomplishments to sharing your values, priorities and

Alan held a unique position in his organization as the Director of Diversity. Part of his responsibility was planning a large recruiting event that demonstrated to high potential recruiting candidates how diversity was valued by the organization. Alan's manager, Pete, was the Vice President of Operations and had risen through the ranks in a combination of positions in sales and technical operations. Pete understood how important Alan's position was within the organization, but he didn't clearly understand how much effort it took to plan the various programs Alan's department hosted. The diversity recruiting dinner took Alan and his staff months to plan and many late nights to make sure the corporate message was conveyed without any hiccups. Pete did not understand how much effort it took to plan this event, nor had Pete ever attended the diversity recruiting dinner.

Planning and executing the diversity recruiting dinner had become a key responsibility and one that was listed as a goal on Alan's performance review. In Alan's first performance review with Pete, Pete wrote *No Information* in the box that would incorporate the diversity recruiting dinner responsibility. Alan was shocked! He'd spent many hours and late nights on the dinner. He had received compliments from across the organization, including the CEO, on what he had accomplished. But Pete had not seen any of it.

Beginning the next day, Alan copied Pete on reports about the events he was planning. He also scheduled monthly meetings so Pete could begin to understand the level of work involved in planning these events. Alan's next performance review had *Exceeds Expectations* in most boxes, including the diversity recruiting dinner. Alan took charge of including Pete in his communications and it changed Pete's perspective, and Alan's performance review, for the better.

Communicate your efforts and influence your review.

goals, communicate as widely as makes strategic sense for the topic. Your manager should not be the only recipient of your communications. Share them with coworkers and managers in other areas or at different levels who may be impacted by your efforts. Share them with others outside your organization who may either be impacted by your efforts or be part of your network. Have your bio or an exposé of your work experience included in your professional association's newsletter.

Refer back to the work you did in Action Box 3 where you identified those who influence your performance review. Communicating widely does not mean sending one email and carbon copying the world. Be strategic in who receives communications from you regarding your performance and which elements of your performance are shared beyond your manager.

Define Your Brand and Promote It

Personal branding is the process by which you market yourself, your skills, talents, accomplishments, values, priorities and goals, to others regardless of whether you know it or take control of it. Others know you in the way you **want** them to know you. Personal branding gives you more control of the perceptions others have about you. It is a process through which you can develop and maintain your personal image. Personal branding impacts not only your performance review, but how you are perceived in all you do throughout the year.

What is your personal brand? How do others perceive you and your work? Just as we discussed previously, perception is reality. It is up to you to affect other people's perception by managing your personal brand. To effectively market yourself, you need to clearly and strategically define your personal brand. Consider the following questions to begin defining your personal brand:

- What is important to you? Do you want to be liked? Respected? Valued? Well paid?

- When people meet you, what is their first impression?

- When people work with you on a project, how do they describe you to others?

- When someone passes you on the street, what is their impression of you?

- What would your closest friends say about you?

- What is it you want people to say about you?

- What do your family members say about you?

- How do you convey your personal brand through your appearance, actions, and communications?

SUCCESS STRATEGY: Steps to Develop Your Personal Brand

1. Know yourself
2. Be genuine in your brand
3. Articulate your brand
4. Promote yourself
5. Manage and nurture your relationships

Know Yourself

The first step to developing your personal brand is to understand yourself and what you want your brand to be. What is core to your personal brand? What do your appearance, actions, activities, relationships, and conversations say about who you are? Reflect again upon the values, priorities, success factors, goals, likes and strengths you defined previously. All of these play an integral part in who you are, and who you want to be. In **Action Box 38**, write down how you want to be perceived.

ACTION BOX 38: Plan Your Personal Brand

Quickly jot down the one or two phrases you want people to use to define you at work. Use the Words to Spark Thoughts at the back of the book if you need some ideas.

Example: Pulled together; Accomplished; Attractive; Intelligent; Well dressed; Balanced; Healthy; A role model; It can be anything!

Be Genuine in Your Brand

How genuine are you? People will eventually see through a façade. Genuinely understanding who you are, what you believe, what you want, and knowing how to communicate it consistently will define your personal brand. It is easier to be true to yourself – to be who you truly are – than to be someone you are not.

I, Tricia, define part of my brand as being a person who shares information freely. I believe that the more people know and share, the better our work will be. When recently encouraged by our administration to limit access to personal calendars (in fact, the new default setting for all staff changed so no one could view any-one else's calendar), I chose to stay true to my brand. I modified my settings to allow others to view my information and shared with my staff that I would continue to remain open with informa-tion. I knew my actions would have no impact on my performance review; it was important for me to stay genuine in my brand and ensure my information continued to be available.

You must be genuine, but you must also be professional. When you start a new position, understanding the environment before you openly express social opinions is the best option. Your appearance, work product, and gestures or actions will reveal a lot about your personal brand initially. Understand your environment before you begin engaging in conversations that might not be appropriate for your particular work environment. Just like any new relationship, you must understand the situation before diving in head first.

> ### SUCCESS STRATEGY: Social Media
>
> People tend to stay true to themselves when using social media. Twitter and Facebook provide a glimpse into the lives of those who use them. Make sure you use social media to communicate your personal brand genuinely and carefully. Social media can show others who you really are and what is important to you, but be careful not to reveal too much or share unprofessional or inappropriate information. Some choose to keep their professional connections confined to LinkedIn and social connections to Facebook to help with these boundaries. Identify your own boundaries and use social media to help define your brand.

Translating your personal brand to your workplace can be challenging. But there are ways to help you determine how to be genuine in your brand.

If you find that your workplace values or priorities and your personal values or priorities are not similar, it can be challenging to be genuine in your brand. You may spend more effort trying to fit in than being yourself. If this is your situation, consider why you were hired for your current position. You might be trying too hard to fit in when you were hired to expand the diversity of the group.

Although a lot of workplace cultures seem to attract similar personalities and skill sets, someone who can be themselves and bring a new perspective to the group can add a lot of value and

Bringing Your Personal Brand to Work

Branding Method	You	Your Environment	Way to Be Genuine
Attire	Business Casual means dress pants and a button up shirt	Business Casual means jeans and a golf shirt	Wear what makes you feel comfortable
Conversations	Don't share much personal information	Everyone seems to know everything about each others' personal lives	Find small ways to share information but maintain the professional line that makes you comfortable
Lunch	Use lunch time for networking and socialization with friends	Your team members eat lunch out together every day	Choose one day a week to network and socialize with your coworkers and explain that you use the other days for professional development
Meeting Participation	Tend to speak up and express your opinion regarding any issue	Meetings seem to be places where decisions are conveyed rather than made	Determine when and how decisions are made, and express your opinions to individuals rather than the group
After Work Socializing	Already have a group of friends and aren't interested in blending business and personal relationships	Coworkers seem to go to happy hours together three or four nights a week	Attend a happy hour every other week to stay current on the office gossip; listen only – don't participate in spreading gossip

perspective. I, Danielle, have been the only professional female in my workplace in many instances. Over the years, I have tried many different strategies to fit into the social interactions of my workplace when this is the case. I have found that being myself works best for me. I can be very good at my job and participate in workplace activities, but excuse myself when the conversation or activities turn to something I am not comfortable participating in.

Articulate Your Brand

To be effective in promoting your personal brand, you must be able to articulate it verbally and nonverbally. Consider what you have defined in the "Know Yourself" step using Action Box 38, and how you can communicate your personal brand through your words and your actions. To be effective, you must know what words to use to clearly define who you are, what you have accomplished or where you want to go in your career.

Methods for Articulating Your Brand

Ideas	Example	Explanation
Incorporate some Action Box 38 information into your standard introduction	Hi! I'm Jack Smith, a collaboration expert at LMN Organization where I am Director of Something	Jack's goal may be that he wants to be known as a collaboration expert. Perhaps a dream job for him is to have his own collaboration consulting company in the future. By including "collaboration expert" in his introduction, people will begin to associate collaboration with Jack. It becomes his brand.
Play the part by dressing for success	While everyone except your manager may go more casual on Fridays or during the summer, you continue to dress business casual each and every day	If you want to be seen as a professional and aspire to the position or level held by your manager, you should play the part. Dress in the same manner as your manager and others at that level. This doesn't mean you alienate yourself from your peers. By remaining consistent in your appearance you develop the personal brand you have planned.
Adjust your written communications	Your emails include a signature block that clearly defines who you are, your current title of Process Engineer and includes a line that says *Project Lead: QRS Project*	If you want to lead more projects or move into positions of greater leadership, showcase that you are currently in a leadership position to all who receive emails from you. This may open up additional opportunities.

Methods for Articulating Your Brand (continued)

Ideas	Example	Explanation
Adjust your verbal communications	Your language is appropriate for the direction you'd like your career to progress toward	Do the words you use convey the image you'd like to portray? Slang terms, profanity, colorful sayings, broken language, and accents all give the listener a mental image of you. This often happens before they actually meet you in person.
Attend conferences and training sessions in areas you'd like to focus on	You use vacation time and spend your own money on training if your employer does not support it	By demonstrating a personal and financial commitment to an endeavor, you let others know how important it is to you.
Let your actions demonstrate your brand	You become involved with a Green Building organization and become certified	Nothing speaks louder than actions. If you aspire to move your career in a more environmentally conscious direction, begin networking with people with the same aspirations. You will feel good about what you are doing, learn a lot and be exposed to career opportunities.

I, Danielle, struggled with incorporating "author" into my personal brand. The work I do through 825 Basics™ and my position as a Vice President in an alternative energy company seemed worlds apart. I found a way to begin incorporating "author" into my engineering world by making it a part of my personal conversations. I practiced the words and phrases I could use in conversation and introductions to articulate "author" in my personal brand. It can still be a struggle to appropriately marry my two worlds, but it is important to incorporate all of me into one package.

Regardless of your methods for articulating your brand, be consistent and genuine. If there is a way to be unique and to stand out from the crowd while remaining professional, then be unique. Your aim is to create a personal brand that over time is memorable and defines who you are. If your brand isn't memorable, then you aren't memorable and that is no way to *Exceed Expectations.*

Promote Yourself

Promoting yourself takes the marketing of your brand one step further. You must promote your brand to your manager, but if you don't promote it to others, you may miss opportunities to achieve your goals or reach your dream job. Promoting yourself includes creating visible value, celebrating accomplishments and strategically communicating your performance. It is about taking all that you know about yourself and putting it out there for others to see, understand and get to know. Broadcast who you are and where you want to go.

I, Tricia, lead a couple of large events outside the scope of my core responsibilities. These events reach a broad audience and benefit the overall organization. After years of going relatively unnoticed or unrecognized, I began to generate final reports at the conclusion of each event. I began to promote myself and the program I lead. I include impact data and highlights from the planning and execution processes. I recognize the other staff involved and explicitly define my leadership role and the leadership role of my team. The reports have ensured a steady flow of compliments for my and our program's compliments bin. By providing the reports, sticking to the data and recognizing the contributions of others, I am viewed as a leader. I am not viewed negatively as a braggart or pushy self-promoter. The reports have heightened the visibility of my program and expanded our leadership role. They provide me with additional opportunities to add value within the overall organization.

Manage and Nurture Your Relationships

Personal branding can only be effective if you have networks and relationships through which you can share your brand. If those you identified previously as your target audience are not part of your current network, identify how to become a part of their network. If the relationships with your manager or others in areas of influence are on shaky ground, open the lines of communication or determine how to strengthen the relationship.

I, Tricia, always send the event final reports I mentioned previously throughout my networks. I include those who are involved or provide support in some way to the events. I show the impact those people have and include them in the recognition. I seek their feedback following the distribution of the final report so they are involved in the process. I assist them with reporting within their own departments so they also have the leadership visibility they deserve. I rely on them to make the events a success. By connecting my success and the success of the events to their leadership and participation, I have developed strong, supporting and reciprocating relationships with them all.

Marketing yourself by sharing your accomplishments and relationships throughout the year can have a lasting impact on your performance review, your career path and your life. As you open the door to your dreams and successes, opportunities will become more visible to you. You will move further along the path to your dream job. Just don't forget to celebrate those accomplishments along the way!

Create Visible Value

Visible value is the contribution you provide to the organization that people can see and quantify. It should tie directly to the organization's goals and priorities. Reflect again on what is important to your organization. In Chapters 4 and 6, you explored your organization's priorities and what performance review success looks like. Both of these are important to consider when evaluating where and how you provide visible value.

Creating Visible Value for Your Organization

Situation	Visible Value	Communication Strategy
Chaired a multi-department leadership conference outside the scope of regular job responsibilities	Over 250 individuals trained on leadership skills while minimizing resource expenditures across multiple departments	The Leadership Conference I chaired this year trained 253 individuals on leadership skills. The 7 participating departments realized a 10% reduction in training costs by participating in the conference.
Project more profitable than expected	75% more profit generated than expected	As a lead on the XYZ project, I'm happy to report that we generated 75% more profit than expected.
Developed new process for proposal submission	Cut staff time by 50% on proposal submission process	I developed a new proposal submission process that has reduced staff time by 50%.
Changed marketing materials	Compliments from 27 customers stating clearer message	The marketing materials I recently modified have been widely complimented. I have received feedback from 27 customers who appreciated the clearer message.
Researched vendors for office supplies	Confirmed we are currently saving 10% over other vendors	The research I completed on the office supply vendors confirmed we are using the most cost effective choice. I have confirmed we are saving 10% over other vendors.

Fundraising is one of my, Tricia's, job responsibilities and core to the university for which I work. In all of my communications to contributors or potential donors, I share how their contributions directly impact students. I share success data and impact stories so the value of the contributions is clearly visible. Contributions to my program appear on financial reports received by other administrators and my management. When I am successful, I can easily showcase the visible value I am providing to my program and my organization. Others can also easily see it within the financial reports, thus creating visible value without my having to explicitly make it visible.

You can highlight your accomplishments and create visible value within your organization through strategic communications to share this information with your manager and others who may influence your performance review.

Your visible value may be in billable hours, direct sales, or meeting project deadlines. It may be showcased in final reports as mentioned previously or in presentations, status reports or your performance review documents such as the Strategies Grid. Use **Action Box 39** to brainstorm ideas on how you can add or showcase visible value to your organization.

ACTION BOX 39: Make Your Visible Value Shine

Given your organization's goals (Action Box 19), describe one or two ways you can provide visible value to the organization.

Example: Goal – To provide superior training to professionals seeking to increase their workplace success and achieve their career goals; Visible value – High ratings from attendees on presentation review forms.

Ensure the value you are contributing is truly visible. You might believe it is obvious, but it may not be so to your manager or others in the organization. Pay attention to the compliments and comments you receive to be sure your contributions are truly visible. If your contributions are obscured, investigate how you can raise the visibility and ensure your manager sees them. Invisible value won't *Exceed Expectations* on a performance review.

Rhonda's group and coworkers are primarily focused on one big project with her manager. However, Rhonda is working on a separate and smaller but equally important project. Initially, Rhonda was disappointed that her manager regularly complimented her coworkers in open forums, but never complimented her. It was particularly disturbing when compliments were given to coworkers who she perceived as much less qualified.

By stepping back and evaluating the situation, Rhonda realized that her manager saw the daily results of her coworkers' efforts, but only saw the large accomplishments she produced. Rhonda participated in the 825 Basics™ class on performance reviews and sent this feedback: "By using the performance review communication tools, I have been very successful in keeping my manager informed of my progress and successes. Now I receive compliments from our manager that let my teammates know I am also contributing to our organization's successes." Rhonda took charge and turned her situation into a positive one.

Out of sight, out of mind – create your own visible value.

I, Danielle, worked for a company that had a great system for recognizing the visible value of each employee. On January 1 each employee was given five recognition cards to use to acknowledge the contributions of fellow employees. When someone received a card, it was proudly displayed so others could see the extra contribution that had been made. We all enjoyed giving and receiving this recognition from our peers. Find a way to recognize people in your workplace.

Seek Opportunities to Shine

Marketing yourself inside and outside your organization and immediate team or department can expand your opportunities. Volunteer for work assignments or take advantage of opportunities within not-for-profits or other volunteer organizations. They can provide the visibility or development opportunities for skills not fully used in your day-to-day job tasks. Participate in outside opportunities to strategically gain experience and advance skills that may help you *Exceed Expectations* on your performance review. Get involved in activities outside of work or in areas of your organization outside of your direct team or department. This will bring opportunities such as future business relationships, job prospects, skills training, professional development, friendships, mentorships, and collaborations in addition to providing visible value.

I, Danielle, was excited when my company agreed to support my participation in the Leadership Texas program. However, a year later when the time came to make the payments, the mood had shifted and support for professional development was no longer available. I had to make the tough decision to pay for the program myself (a $10,000 plus commitment) or forfeit my position in the program. I decided to make the investment in myself. Two years later, a friendship I had developed in the Leadership Texas program led to a great new job opportunity. I was glad I had taken advantage of a professional development opportunity and used it to promote my personal brand.

Choosing an opportunity to shine requires a commitment to the new venture. If you join an extracurricular activity to demonstrate or grow your skills, you are making an impression on a new

Irene was responsible for a particular subset of her team's project. She didn't manage people and was not in charge of budgeting, two key job experiences needed for advancement or for other external job opportunities. Through her volunteer efforts, she was able to manage large teams, coordinate communications across the country, develop and manage a budget, write grant proposals and raise funds.

When an amazing job opportunity became available that matched Irene's motivations and aligned with her dream job aspirations, she was able to get the job based on her volunteer experiences. Budgeting, fundraising and management were all required experiences for the job. Had she solely relied on her paid job experiences, she would not have been qualified, but with her volunteer experiences, the opportunity became available and her experiences led to both landing the amazing job and *Exceeding Expectations* on her first performance review.

All experiences add value. Learn how to communicate them.

group of people. Make sure you dedicate yourself to the commitment and continue to be genuine in your brand.

I, Tricia, have recently taken on the role of volunteer coordinator for a local engineering outreach not-for-profit. Many of my friends and coworkers might think I'm crazy for taking on this role; however, I know it aligns with the work I am doing and the services I am providing at the university. The role allows me to make connections with engineers and organizations across my community. Not only does my role as coordinator support the local organization, but it provides me a network of potential mentors or volunteers for my university programs. I am able to showcase my skills and bring visibility to the work I am doing outside of the university environment.

SUCCESS STRATEGY: Choosing an Opportunity to Shine

Things to consider when choosing an extracurricular activity to showcase your skills or expand opportunities:

- Your ability to commit to the position – disappointing your co-volunteers could be detrimental
- Why you want to participate – your goal should help determine the activity to which you commit
- Time requirement of the activity – some activities require weekly commitments for a year, others may only last a weekend; decide ahead if you can commit to a one-time event or ongoing activity
- Goals for growth of position – discern if you would you like to advance to President of the organization or serve in a support role
- How the activity will be perceived by your employer – if you work for a very conservative company and choose to become the local Democratic Party representative, it could be a conflict

Share and Celebrate Your Accomplishments

You have probably heard the age-old question, "If a tree falls in the forest and no one is around to hear it, does it make a sound?" Perhaps the same question could be asked about your accomplishments, "If you accomplish something but no one is around to see it, did you actually accomplish something of value?" It is important to share your accomplishments and successes at your performance review **and** when they occur throughout the year.

Celebrating accomplishments is an effective way to communicate them to others. It increases the visibility of the value you are contributing to your organization. Sometimes it may feel like bragging to share your accomplishments widely; celebrating accomplishments and sharing in the celebration can remove the bragging perception and showcase how you *Exceed Expectations* in your job.

Michael worked for a technology company and his location was fortunate to be the last in the country to open a very prestigious demonstration center for high-profile customer visits. Michael and his team had the good fortune of flying to all the other centers in the U.S. and exploring what was good/bad, right/wrong, and so on. When it opened, Michael's center was topnotch with no detail spared. Future demonstration center funding was divided based on the ratings of the centers, and Michael's boss wanted as large of a portion of the pie as he could get.

Michael's demonstration center started the year by inviting the entire sales force for a tour and an audio/visual presentation to make sure they were properly impressed. During the presentation, Michael's team told their guests that they expected a rating of 10 on each and every encounter with the center, wanting to fix anything that would prevent a 10 before the visitors completed surveys. Throughout the year, as clients were using the center, Michael's team members would pass the clients in the hall and ask "How are we doing? Are we still a 10?" The clients did not have any reason to give a rating of less than 10 on each and every visit. Sure enough, the center received a perfect 10 average by the end of the year. Michael's team and center got the lion's share of the funding and were the envy of every center in the country!

Ask for feedback, and the perfect score.

There are easy ways to celebrate and share your accomplishments with others:

- Let's grab lunch and celebrate sending a great proposal out to the client.

- I passed my licensing exam. Drinks on me tonight.

- My paper was accepted for presentation at the national conference. I'm so excited that I am going to reward myself with a first class plane ticket.

- We did an exceptional job on the ABC project. My skills have grown greatly as a leader throughout.

- I just saved the company hundreds of customer complaints by fixing this problem. We all just got our weekends back!

You need to take a step back from the daily grind and recognize when you have met your milestones or accomplished your goals. Celebrating can rejuvenate your spirit and remind you of the happiness of success. Take time to celebrate your accomplishments to both *Exceed Expectations* in your job and in your life.

Jacob is a mid-level manager who works for a technology company. He has always been driven to earn the highest possible score on performance reviews. This drive has always earned him a perfect rating and flattering performance reviews; however, Jacob never got invited on the exclusive award trips that a few of the high performers went on each year.

After a few years of feeling left out, Jacob took one of the high performers who was included in the trips out to lunch to ask why this seemed to happen. Jacob learned that the spaces are very limited. There are always far more worthy recipients than slots and each candidate must fight for the invitations. This coworker told Jacob that at the beginning of each year he always told his boss he wanted to go on that trip and reminded him frequently throughout the year. Every time kudos were sent to this coworker, he would forward them to his boss along with a note "justification for the award trip." If someone gave the coworker verbal kudos, he kindly asked them to put the compliment in writing. This seemed very awkward to Jacob. He was not used to tooting his own horn and had trusted that others would see his good work. Jacob decided to take the coworker's advice and tried this method. Jacob has since been invited on the award trip every year.

Take control! Ask for what you want.

Connect to the Strategies Grid

A challenge many people face is focusing too much on one area of your job that you consider to be the highest priority. If you do this, you will probably have 20 accomplishments listed in a single area. *Exceeding Expectations* on your overall review requires that you demonstrate accomplishment in all job responsibilities.

After collecting your accomplishments and communicating them strategically to your target audience, it is time to connect them to your job responsibilities in the Strategies Grid. Align your accomplishments to your strategic job responsibilities. Clearly show where you meet or exceed your goals or objectives. Share compliments you receive as examples of your success. Don't hesitate to include anticipated accomplishments as well to highlight progress and future anticipated success. Ensure you document accomplishments that showcase how you *Exceed Expectations.* Use **Action Box 40** to align your accomplishments with job responsibilities.

As you continue to build your final Strategies Grid, you have likely created a chart with multiple goals or objectives for each job responsibility. Additionally, you will likely find that you have multiple accomplishments for each goal or objective and job responsibility. Capture all of these in your Strategies Grid in the way that best works for you. Multiple table cells or bullets for each accomplishment may make it easier.

ACTION BOX 40: Connect Accomplishments to Job Responsibilities

Make the connections to the Strategies Grid and your performance review process. What accomplishments do you have for each job responsibility?

Strategy 1	Strategy 2	Strategy 3
Job Responsibilities	Goals or Objectives	Accomplishments
Example: Perform annual facility audits to ensure compliance with regulations.	Example: Complete 100% of audits in fiscal year.	Example: Completed 100% of audits, sharing best practices to improve processes at 50% of facilities.

Chapter 11 Takeaways

Communicate Your Accomplishments

- You must develop a personal marketing strategy to communicate your personal brand.

- Look for opportunities to showcase your personal brand inside and outside of your organization.

- Communicate your efforts and influence your review.

- Accomplishments must be shared and celebrated to be appreciated.

- Visible value yields results and recognition.

- All experiences add value. Learn how to communicate them.

- Take control! Ask for feedback, and the perfect score.

Identify and Address Challenges

Strategies Grid

Strategy 1	Strategy 2	Strategy 3	Strategy 4	Strategy 5
Job Responsibilities	Goals or Objectives	Accomplishments	Challenges	Success Methods

Regardless of your situation and no matter how deeply you understand your environment, expectations and responsibilities, you will inevitably encounter challenges. Challenges may be internal and related to your skills, abilities, knowledge, timelines or resources; or external, such as an industry downturn, competing interests or new technologies. Identifying and addressing challenges enables you to stay relevant in the work that you do.

CHAPTER 12

Challenges

"*Opportunity is missed by most people because it is dressed in overalls and looks like work.*"

Thomas A. Edison, American Inventor, Scientist and Businessman

Throughout the year, it is useful to step back and do a bit of research to ensure your personal brand and your strategic communications are having the results you desire. Investigate how you are being perceived by your manager, teammates, coworkers and peers. Observe what job responsibility or workplace opportunities and threats pose challenges. This personal research may identify hidden challenges that could otherwise have surprised you in a performance review, thwarting your ability to *Exceed Expectations*.

Opportunities and Threats

While it is important to understand the internal system and yourself, to thrive in your work environment and *Exceed Expectations* on your performance review you should be aware of opportunities and threats that may pose challenges. Are there opportunities in your workplace to showcase your strengths and move you closer to your lifetime goals? Are there threats that you need to be aware of and observe to ascertain whether adjustments in your communications or performance are warranted? It is easy to be busy with your day-to-day job, plowing away without lifting your head to see what is going on around you. When you do not take time to observe your environment for both opportunities and threats, you can be blindsided in your performance review. Someone else may get that awesome opportunity you wanted or, in the worst case scenario, your job may be eliminated.

Take a few minutes to brainstorm current opportunities and threats in your workplace. **Action Box 41** provides some examples and space to write it all down.

Opportunities and threats can sometimes be the same; you must be aware of both. Ensure communications with your manager highlight your strengths so that you will be considered for and can take advantage of opportunities while avoiding any

---

ACTION BOX 41: Analyze Your Workplace Opportunities and Threats

Opportunities
Example: New manager; New project; Department restructuring; Increased budget; An acquisition by the company

Threats
Example: Decreased budget; Lost client; New manager; Department restructuring; Economic conditions; Social shifts

---

negative impact from threats. Opportunities don't just happen. You must create your own opportunities by communicating your goals, strengths, values and priorities to your manager and others throughout your organization and overcoming challenges.

Keep in mind that sometimes opportunities and threats are outside of your control. You may not be in a position to take advantage of all opportunities or perhaps politics or bureaucracy come into play. Threats also may appear suddenly, providing you little time to react and adjust. The key is to be prepared to the best of your ability so that, for the majority of situations, you can remain in the driver's seat.

Direct Conversations

One of the best ways to receive feedback on your personal brand or any opportunities or threats in the workplace is to have a direct conversation with your manager and others in your target audience. Directly ask your manager how you are doing and what the perception is about your work or your workplace environment:

- How do you feel I am performing on this project? In what areas would you like to see improvement?

- One of my goals is to *Exceed Expectations* on my performance review this year. Are there some areas I need to improve upon to achieve that rating?

- Are there areas in which I should focus my skills development and training on this year?

Receiving feedback throughout the year about these perceptions enhances the regular strategic communications you provide to your manager. Keep in mind, though, that you may have a manager who is not skilled at providing feedback.

I, Tricia, had a manager that skirted the issue whenever I directly asked about my performance. He would always answer about my team and not my personal performance. I could never get a sense of what I needed to improve upon in my performance, while I kept trying.

> **SUCCESS STRATEGY: Taking Notes**
>
> When you have direct conversations with your manager, take notes. When you refer back to the notes, there will be items you forgot about or might interpret differently after reflecting on them. Often, a dedicated notebook or folder will help you keep these conversations organized so they are easy to use in future conversations, or when performance evaluation time arrives.

If you are able to get direct feedback, be sure to incorporate any challenges outlined by your manager in your Strategies Grid. Address the challenges directly and describe how you are going to improve or eliminate them. Take control of your performance review by turning a challenge into a possible future accomplishment.

I, Tricia, was asked once by a manager, "What is your problem?" That isn't the type of question you want to get from a manager. I was new to the position and needed this direct conversation to improve my performance. My manager shared that others did not want to work with me as I continually criticized their work and didn't seem like a team player. This was shocking to me as I had always felt that I aimed to improve the processes in place and work collaboratively to accomplish our goals. My challenge was that in this new environment, people expected personal relationships and respect for the historical way things had been done. I was there to get the job done and improve the process. This approach didn't work and I needed to modify my methods. My suggestions for improvements were perceived as criticisms and, worse yet, personal attacks. I began to take the time to get to know my coworkers on a personal level and worked on the relationships. Eventually, I was able to improve processes and move us closer to our goals. It took longer than I'd wanted, but this work environment required relationship building to take place along the way. My direct conversation with my manager gave me the feedback I needed to succeed.

360 Degree Feedback

Many organizations have some sort of peer review or 360 degree feedback process in place to assist with performance reviews. A 360 degree feedback process solicits feedback from your circumference of coworkers, employees and managers. It is designed to view all aspects of your work from different perspectives. Regardless of whether your organization has a formal 360 degree feedback system, you can solicit your own 360 degree feedback. Understanding how your peers perceive your work and performance can provide great insight into your personal brand. It also can provide eye-opening insights about your career and your performance that you may have never considered.

May works for an organization that incorporates a 360 degree feedback process into the formal performance review process once an employee has reached management level. The 360 degree reviews were not incorporated into the formal rankings, but the results were compiled and shared for personal and career development. May was very excited to have been promoted to manager and was looking forward to the feedback she would receive in the 360 degree review process. She was often being complimented by coworkers and her manager for her performance and management skills, so she was confident it would all be great feedback.

When the results came back, one comment particularly took her by surprise. A coworker had commented, "She tends to do the fun stuff first instead of working on the higher priority tasks." May knew this was true, but had not realized how transparent it was. As a result, May paid close attention to her work processes – which tasks she jumped right on and which tasks she waited on or tried to avoid. This provided great insight into her career aspirations and motivations. May still looks forward to the 360 degree feedback and continues to adjust her work processes to ensure the high-priority work receives earlier and more visible attention. The fun work also gets done, just with less fanfare.

Perception is reality, become more aware of coworkers or others' perceptions.

Refer back to those influencers you defined in Strategy 1. Who can provide you with the 360 degree feedback you need to improve? Create your own 360 degree feedback form or use your organization's official process. You can ask the same questions you would ask your manager in a direct conversation. Invite someone to lunch and ask for feedback on your performance, projects or other characteristics of your personal brand. Set up one-on-one meetings with your peers or other influences to solicit feedback.

It is up to you to be sure you get the feedback you need to *Exceed Expectations* in all your strategic job responsibilities.

I, Danielle, have never had a formal 360 degree review, however, a friend once told me to never eat lunch alone. I had assumed the result would be a better network. The bigger result was feedback on my work activities and understanding the politics in my workplace. I was able to glean an informal 360 degree feedback from daily lunch conversations with coworkers.

Use **Action Box 42** to brainstorm who can provide you with 360 degree feedback on your performance. Consider how you can go about soliciting this feedback from your coworkers, employees and/or manager throughout the year.

ACTION BOX 42: Identify Sources for Your 360 Degree Feedback

Who can provide you 360 degree feedback and how can you go about getting it from him/her/them?

Example: Jason – volunteer peer, Alexis – team member, Robin – past manager, Juanita – coworker; Set up online survey and ask each to complete anonymously

Personal Board of Directors

A personal board of directors consists of your mentors who are those go-to career people. They can serve as advocates for your performance and can provide you with the feedback you need to enhance your performance or promote your accomplishments. They can help you stay aware of the opportunities and threats related to your job responsibilities, workplace or industry. The people who make up your personal board of directors may be within your company or outside your industry. They are part of the networks you identified in Strategy 1.

Your personal board of directors can provide direct feedback and guidance for your personal success and top-ranking performance. They can hold you accountable to your goals and help you correct your course or perceptions, should your career or personal brand drift. They can also help you communicate your accomplishments and shine light on the work that you do.

I, Tricia, have a group of friends I can depend on for direct feedback and guidance. I don't call them a personal board of directors, but I know they will help provide me perspective or insights when needed. When I was offered my first position at the university, I was hesitant to consider the possibility. I would be leaving my well-paid and advancing job as an engineer and staff positions at universities tend to be less lucrative and more limiting. I was focused on the pay and the advancement limitations of the offered position. When a good friend and mentor said, "But you have to take the job! It's the Tricia job." That is when I realized that pay and a defined career path for advancement were not the most important aspects to me. Being in a job I loved and having the opportunity to make a difference in the lives of students every day was more important. My friend's perspective provided me with the awakening I needed to realize that I'd forever regret not taking that step. I am thankful to my mentor, husband and all the others who made sure I took the "Tricia job" at the university.

Barry served in a number of volunteer roles within his organization, contributing to the organization's community service and recruiting goals. After moving to a new department, he continued these volunteer roles. When he began his new position, Barry felt his volunteer roles were known and accepted by his new manager and peers.

A couple of people on Barry's personal board of directors were connected to both the leaders in his new department and the leaders in the departments in which he volunteered. Through these relationships, Barry learned that his new manager halted a bonus he should have received for his volunteer efforts, and was limiting his opportunities in the organization. It became clear that Barry would never *Exceed Expectations* in this situation, or receive the recognition and opportunities he deserved. Barry was grateful to his personal board of directors for opening his eyes to the situation and encouraging him to pursue other opportunities. Barry quickly found an opportunity outside the organization and is much happier in a position where he is valued.

Create a personal board of directors who will give you honest feedback and insight while keeping you connected to your personal brand.

I, Danielle, have been fortunate that my career has taken many paths. Some of these paths have taken me into great situations; others have not been as good. Now when I begin a new adventure, I let my personal board of directors know what my objectives are in the new role. They keep me on track and remind me of my personal goals when I lose sight of my direction. These honest reminders have greatly enhanced my career and have helped me stay on track to accomplish my goals.

Take a few minutes to name your personal board of directors in **Action Box 43**. Consider who helps you now and who provides feedback on your performance and career. Think of who knows

---

ACTION BOX 43: Identify Your Personal Board of Directors

Name your personal board of directors. Who helps you now and provides the feedback you need?

Example: Rod, Angel, Juan, Olatha, Samantha

Who do you need to add to your advocates? With whom should you develop a deeper relationship?

Example: Adelle – need manager's perspective; Tony – great networker and can share tips

---

the **real you** and understands your goals. Decide if there are others within your networks with whom you would like to develop a deeper relationship. Consider others who may be able to fill in the gaps and provide you with feedback on other areas of your job.

Observations

In addition to receiving direct feedback from others, it is important to continually make observations about how you are being perceived and what is happening in your work environment. Pay attention to the compliments and comments, indirect or casual feedback, you receive to see if they reflect your desired personal brand. Examples of such are a "Thanks, this is perfect!" reply to an informational email you sent or a "You were so prepared today." comment you received on the way out of a meeting. Strategy 1 was all about paying attention to and understanding yourself and your environment. It is important these observations and reflections continue year round to move your performance review, personal brand and career in the direction you desire.

Connect Challenges to the Strategies Grid

The opportunities, threats and challenges you identify may tie to job responsibilities or impact accomplishing your goals. Feedback you receive regarding your workplace environment or personal brand may illuminate challenges related to your job responsibilities. If so, be sure to connect them in the Strategies Grid. Address challenges directly.

Align Challenges to Goals

Goals	Challenges
Meet organizational goals of 85% employee retention and 75% excellent ratings on customer service	Merger of company with another industry leader has led to significantly lower retention rates than goal
Expand market share by 5%	New product introduced by competitor has greatly expanded market potential and diluted our market share, making it more difficult to increase the overall market share
Host 2 events for our customers and employees to share new technology	Budgetary constraints have limited the number of customers who can travel to event
Attend 2 training classes to advance technical knowledge	Budget only allows for attendance at one training class
Reduce office supply budget by 30%	Expanded staff has increased number of people using supplies; although pricing for supplies has been negotiated for lower rates, more supplies are being purchased

Regardless of how you learned about the challenge or collected the feedback, incorporate it into the Strategies Grid as a proactive step toward your personal development. In Strategy 5 you will be able to address the challenge and turn it into a future success and accomplishment, but first you need to use **Action Box 44** to tie your challenges to your job responsibilities.

ACTION BOX 44: Connect Challenges to Job Responsibilities

Make the connections to the Strategies Grid and your performance review process. What challenges, if any, do you have for each job responsibility?

Strategy 1	Strategy 2	Strategy 4
Job Responsibilities	Goals and Objectives	Challenges
Example: Ensure 24 hour response time to all customer inquiries	Example: All customer inquiries are responded to within 24 hours as measured by electronic response system.	Example: Staff turnover has required me to work overtime to meet this goal
		Example: I am no longer being challenged by long-term project work as I am now consumed by short-term and redundant inquiries

Just as with goals and objectives, you may have multiple challenges for each job responsibility in your Strategies Grid. You may even have multiple challenges for each goal or objective. Your Strategies Grid must work for you – use multiple table cells or bullets for each challenge to help make it easier.

Perhaps you will need to better develop a certain skill to *Exceed Expectations*. Perhaps you need a different timeline or additional resources. Identifying, understanding and then communicating challenges ensure your rating is not jeopardized by a misunderstanding, misinformation or unrealistic expectations. By identifying the challenges, you create a path to implementing success methods in Strategy 5. You move toward *Exceeding Expectations* in all your job responsibilities.

Chapter 12 Takeaways

Challenges

- Opportunities and threats can catch you off-guard in a performance review. Know what yours are.

- Perception is reality, become more aware of coworkers or others' perceptions.

- Create a personal board of directors who will give you honest feedback and insight while keeping you connected to your personal brand.

- Use direct conversations, 360 degree feedback, a personal board of directors and observations to ensure you are *Exceeding Expectations*.

Implement Success Methods

Strategies Grid

Strategy 1	Strategy 2	Strategy 3	Strategy 4	Strategy 5
Job Responsibilities	Goals or Objectives	Accomplishments	Challenges	Success Methods

Throughout this book, you have focused on creating strategic communications and translating your accomplishments and job performance successes into visible value. You now have the framework and our Balanced Model to *Exceed Expectations* on your next performance review. The final strategy takes this framework and turns it into an Action Plan. Annual updates of this Action Plan will have you *Exceeding Expectations* throughout your career. Creating a success method involves aiming for the future, defining a plan and putting it all into action. It takes your job responsibility and connects it through the Strategies Grid to where you want to go and the dream job you know is out there waiting for you.

CHAPTER 13

Complete the Strategies Grid

"Nothing can add more power to your life than concentrating all your energies on a limited set of targets."

Nido Qubein, Leadership Expert

Y ou have researched and defined the performance review process, your environment and what success means for you. You investigated your dream job and your goals. You learned how to create alignments with your manager's and organization's values and priorities. You have the information you need to complete the Strategies Grid and take your next step toward performance review success.

Summarize the Research

To move this research into action, compile the information you have collected, brainstormed and documented throughout the book in **Action Box 45**. Use it to house all the information in one place so that you can begin to investigate trends, alignments and disconnects.

People often have difficulties identifying trends for themselves. If necessary, reach out to your personal board of directors to help you find trends and connection points throughout the exercises. Sometimes that objective outsider will more easily identify those areas of disconnect, improvement or success.

When I, Tricia, was considering a job offer at a university, my mentor had told me, "It's the Tricia job." She was able to help me evaluate my motivations, values, priorities, likes and dislikes. She knew I was most successful in those areas more closely related to the job responsibilities of this opportunity. She saw the trends in my work, volunteer roles and successes, and was able to provide the objective assessment I needed.

I have been able to continue to assess my trends throughout my career. I know my performance *Exceeds Expectations* when my work is process oriented and I am able to be a collaborative leader. I tailor my communications and success methods to embrace my strengths with my goals in mind.

ACTION BOX 45: Summarize Your Research

Compile your notes, sketches, and exercise answers. What trends do you see throughout what you have discovered?

Action Box	Action Box	Your Notes or Conclusions
Past Performance Reviews – What were the attributes of your best reviews?	2 Chapter 3	
Priorities – What did you discover about your priorities compared to those of your manager and organization?	11 Chapter 4	
Success – What does success look like for your performance review considering your definition and that of your manager and organization?	14 15 16 Chapter 6	
Likes and Dislikes – What did you discover about your job preferences?	21 Chapter 8	
Compliments and Comments – What did you learn about your strengths, what others think about your performance, and what you can do to influence perceptions?	24 27 Chapter 8	
Dream Job – How can you incorporate your dream job into your communications and your career plan?	28 Chapter 9	
Opportunities and Threats – What can you take advantage of to *Exceed Expectations* in your next review?	41 Chapter 12	

Your success methods are derived from the trends you identified in Action Box 45 (Summarize the Research) as well as the challenges identified in Action Box 44 (Connect Challenges to Job Responsibilities). Success methods are individual and need to reflect your personal brand. Consider how you can address the challenges and trends throughout the year in preparation for your performance review. How can you modify your strategic communications to move you closer to your definition of success? Success methods are different for every person and showcase your problem-solving and strategic-planning abilities. You need to capitalize on your strengths to define your success methods for each job responsibility.

Connect Success Methods to Trends

The trends you identified in Action Box 45 (Summarize the Research) describe how you perform best and give insights into your success methods. Success methods highlight your strengths and capitalize on the positive outcomes of the trends you have identified. You may share your ambitions by explaining how you would like to grow a given job responsibility. You also may simply explain that your future plan is to continue to *Exceed Expectations* in that responsibility area. At a minimum, you demonstrate responsibility, ambition, and that you are focused on succeeding.

Based on your trends, what success methods have you identified? Have you identified new strategies on how to communicate

Align Success Methods to Trends

Trend	Success Method
Silent leader – Performs best in the background	• Provide written and thorough updates to your manager detailing accomplishments • Identify times when it is more appropriate to communicate or promote yourself verbally • Draft language to use in these situations and practice saying them daily to become more comfortable
Strong communicator and people person; performs best in front of a crowd	• Recognize opportunities to showcase others • Use communication skills to better promote personal successes • Identify opportunities to promote organization through networking and public speaking
Performs best as a technical leader	• Write articles for industry publications to highlight work • Offer brown-bag training programs to share knowledge with coworkers, customers or vendors • Expand technical knowledge in a specific area
Performs best when organized	• Establish electronic filing system to enhance ease of use by team • Take on additional responsibility because organization allows for more efficient work • Promote organization as a skill and demonstrate to others how it makes you a better employee
Needs new direction – performance will be improved with change in work	• Communicate desire to manager, coworkers or network about the specific qualities you want in a next position • Identify positions that contain dream job aspects • Identify current job responsibilities that can fulfill needs for now
Enjoys change – perform best with variety	• Communicate to manager and coworkers your desire to work on a variety of small projects versus one long, large project • Review Action Box exercises regularly to identify changes in your career desires • Become aware of small changes in your current situation that will meet this desire
Influential – perform best when able to influence and lead	• Develop ways to use your influence to bring in new customers • Share the breadth of your circle of influence with your manager, coworkers, and employees so they can use your strength • Mentor others in your organization on how to network to develop strong, influential relationships

about your performance? Do you have strengths you need to focus on in a more strategic manner throughout all your job responsibilities? Use **Action Box 46** to identify success methods based on your trends.

ACTION BOX 46: Connect Success Methods to Trends

Using your trends identified in Action Box 45, write down success methods that will help you reach the *Exceeds Expectations* rating on your performance review.

Examples are provided on page 215.

Connect Success Methods to Job Responsibilities

In Strategy 4 you identified job responsibility challenges and some means to address them. To be successful in your performance review, you must connect your job responsibilities and challenges to success methods. You should incorporate all you have learned about yourself, your personal brand, your goals, your values and your priorities into your success methods and use them as a means to further your goals and showcase your performance excellence.

I, Danielle, love travelling for business and pleasure. While in a previous job that required a significant amount of travel, I had my first child. Traveling four days a week no longer aligned with my personal goal of being able to spend time each day with my son. My challenge became limiting my travel while still successfully accomplishing my job responsibilities. The success method I developed was to use technology and new programs to vastly reduce the amount of travel required for my position. I presented this to my manager but, unfortunately, he was not receptive to the idea. For my manager, travel was integral to the success method for my job responsibilities. For me to be successful and *Exceed Expectations* with my manager, I was going to have to travel and go against my personal goals. I was prepared for my review, and just as discussed in Chapter 2, I was prepared to respond when my manager surprised me with his comments. I transitioned to a position within the company where my success methods could be aligned with my personal goals.

Align Success Methods to Challenges

Challenges	Success Methods
Budget too small for project	Develop a spreadsheet with breakdown of specific costs to determine exactly where budget was constrained, then work to find more cost-effective ways to manage those areas
Not enough employees available to complete project on time	Explore options for contract employees to complete portions of project or explain modifications to the timeline given the number of employees available
Merger of company with another industry leader has led to significantly lower retention rates than goal	Develop team building program to unite merged employees and ask senior management to talk with employees about the future of the company
	Shift some of the training budget to areas for employee retention and present data to demonstrate why turnover was so high
New product introduced by competitor has greatly expanded market potential and diluted market share, making it more difficult to increase the overall market share	Present data demonstrating percentages prior to introduction of new product and post introduction, then develop marketing materials for expanding customer base in new market areas
Budgetary constraints have limited the number of customers who can travel to event	Implement web-based training technology to host event electronically
Budget only allows for attendance at one training class	Find local or self-study training mechanisms to expand knowledge
Expanded staff has increased the number and cost of supplies even though pricing for supplies had been negotiated for lower rates	Breakdown data on a cost-per-employee basis to demonstrate cost savings, and implement awareness program to remind employees how much supplies cost, such as think twice before printing

Job responsibility challenges come in many forms, but they are often related to budgetary or workplace constraints. In these instances, you will need to develop success methods to overcome or address the difficulties you face.

Once you have considered success methods for your job responsibilities and challenges, it is time to complete the Strategies Grid. You will connect the success methods identified based on your trends and those based on your job responsibility challenges. Use **Action Box 47** to connect your strategic job responsibilities to success methods you have identified.

ACTION BOX 47: Connect Success Methods to Job Responsibilities

Using your strategic job responsibilities and challenges, write down success methods that will help you reach the *Exceeds Expectations* rating on your performance review.

Strategies Grid

Strategy 1	Strategy 4	Strategy 5
Job Responsibilities	Challenges	Success Methods
Example: Increase sales by 15% of Widget 423	*Example: Sales in third quarter trend downward*	*Example: Identify opportunities to promote organization through networking and public speaking opportunities*

Your Completed Strategies Grid

You should now have the information to complete your Strategies Grid. Combine the information you have entered into Action Boxes connecting the other strategies to job responsibilities: 32 (Personal Goals), 33 (Job Specific Goals), 40 (Accomplishments), 44 (Challenges) and 47 (Success Methods). Use the blank Strategies Grid provided in **Action Box 48** to collect your information. Review and revise to ensure the Strategies Grid meets your performance review needs. Make sure the information flows and makes sense from one strategy to the next for each job responsibility.

Managing your performance review is a continual process tied with your career development strategy and your goals. Take control of your performance review and your career by defining your strategy to *Exceed Expectations*. The completed Strategies Grid is your tool for strategically documenting your job responsibilities and accomplishments. It is your tool for communicating about your performance to your manager and will be a continual work in progress. Your final step to take control of your performance review is to define your Performance Review Action Plan, how you will implement your Strategies Grid.

ACTION BOX 48: Complete Your Strategies Grid

Job Responsibilities	Goals or Objectives	Accomplishments	Challenges	Success Methods
Example: Manage four projects	Example: Within budget	Example: Managed three projects within budget	Example: Budge restraints	Example: Expand both scope and budget responsibilities of future projects

I will review and update my Strategies Grid _____
(insert timeframe such as weekly, monthly, quarterly).

Chapter 13 Takeaways

Complete the Strategies Grid

- Success methods showcase your problem-solving and strategic-planning abilities.

- Capitalize on your strengths to define success methods for each job responsibility.

- Manage your performance review continually.

- Your Strategies Grid documents and communicates your job responsibilities and accomplishments.

CHAPTER 14

Implement Your Strategy

"Never confuse motion with action."

Benjamin Franklin, Inventor

Your Performance Review Action Plan defines your personal approach to performance review success. It takes your Strategies Grid and implements your plan, putting it into motion. Action planning is one of the best methods you can use to accomplish your goals and achieve success. If you write your goals using the SMART methodology discussed in Chapter 9 and include milestones for your goals, action planning will easily follow. Action planning takes your goals and milestones, prioritizes them, and decides the order in which you will move strategically forward, with your lifetime goals in constant view.

By creating a Performance Review Action Plan, you create a means for addressing the total environment you have defined and the actions you have identified to move you toward a top rating. As you have progressed through this book, you have created the framework for your Action Plan. You have detailed the strategies you need to implement to *Exceed Expectations* on your performance review and reach your career goals.

Steps to Successful Action Planning

There are five basic steps to successful action planning, beginning with writing it down. Writing your Action Plan down makes it real and provides a visible and specific timeline of what you are doing and where you want to go.

By creating specific and timely actions and tasks, you start to visualize your plan for achieving success. Writing it down helps you to hold yourself accountable and take action.

Sharing your Action Plan with others increases your accountability by providing an opportunity for others to remind you of your timelines, assist you along the way, and provide feedback or gentle nudges to keep you moving toward your goals. Be strategic with whom you share your Performance Review Action Plan and consider your personal board of directors as a valuable resource.

Finally, action planning should be considered a continual process where you review, revise and celebrate along the way. Your Action Plan is a dynamic, living document. Your goals, values, priorities, or environment may change and your Action Plan must be continually modified to reflect your situation.

> **Success Strategy: Steps to Successful Action Planning**
> 1. Write it down
> 2. Be specific and timely
> 3. Share it with others
> 4. Review it and revise it
> 5. Celebrate successes

Begin Your Action Plan

To begin your Action Plan in preparation for your performance review, note when your next review will be in **Action Box 49**, then review each of the exercises you've worked through and mark in the box those you need to spend more time reviewing or completing. Evaluate the exercises described throughout the book and how they may affect your performance rating. We have assumed that you have worked through the Action Boxes in this book as you have read it; however, these exercises require reflection and you may have a different perspective on what you have written after reflecting on it for awhile.

Finish the Action Box 49 chart by prioritizing the exercises and actions you have indicated and setting target dates for completion. You may want to prioritize the exercises you have yet to fully complete; however, you may have discovered one of the areas where you could easily begin to apply your performance review strategies. You may just decide to start with that one area and finish the others later. You know your environment and your performance review goals, and you must create an Action Plan that works for

ACTION BOX 49: Complete Step 1 of Your Performance Review Action Plan

My next performance review will occur: _____
(insert month or specific date).

Action Box	Need More Review	High Priority	Target Date
Chapter 1-The Balanced Model			
1: Write Your Strategic Communications Goal			
Chapter 3-Understand the Performance Review Process			
2: Assess Past Performance Reviews			
3: Explore Your Performance Review Process			
4: Identify Your Manager's Performance Review Style			
5: Describe Your Manager's Influencers			
6: Identify Valued Peer Skills			
7: Describe Your Organization's Rating Structure			
Chapter 4-Explore Workplace Priorities			
8: Recognize Your Workplace Priorities			
9: Note Your Manager's Priorities			
10: Describe Your Organization's Priorities			
11: Compare Priorities			
Chapter 5-Explore External Performance Review Influences			
12: Examine Your External Network			
13: Identify External Network Needs			
Chapter 6-Define Performance Review Success Grid			
14: Describe Your Idea of Performance Review Success			
15: Define Your Manager's Performance Review Success			
16: Define Your Organization's Performance Review Success			

ACTION BOX 49: Complete Step 1 of Your Performance Review Action Plan Continued…

Action Box	Need More Review	High Priority	Target Date
Strategy 1-Understand Job Responsibilities			
Chapter 7-Define Your Job			
17: List Your Official Job Responsibilities			
18: Write Your Current Job Responsibilities			
19: Define Your Organization's Goals and/or Mission			
20: Rewrite to Identify Strategic Job Responsibilities			
Strategy 2-Define Goals or Objectives			
Chapter 8-Reveal the Real You			
21: List Your Likes and Dislikes			
22: Identify Your Strengths			
23: Align Your Strengths Strategically			
24: List Compliments			
25: List Your Weaknesses			
26: Address Your Weaknesses			
27: Record Comments			
Chapter 9-Define Your Goals			
28: Identify Your Dream Job			
29: Define Your Lifetime Goals			
30: Define Your Five-Year Goals			
31: Define Your One-Year Goals			
32: Connect Personal Goals to Job Responsibilities			
33: Connect Job Specific Goals to Job Responsibilities			

ACTION BOX 49: Complete Step 1 of Your Performance Review Action Plan Continued…

Action Box	Need More Review	High Priority	Target Date
Strategy 3-Collect and Communicate Accomplishments			
Chapter 10-Collect Your Accomplishments			
34: Plan Your Accomplishments Reservoir(s)			
35: Plan Your Kind Words and Compliments Bin(s)			
36: Make Your CV Action Plan			
37: Make Your Resume Action Plan			
Chapter 11-Communicate Your Accomplishments			
38: Plan Your Personal Brand			
39: Make Your Visible Value Shine			
40: Connect Accomplishments to Job Responsibilities			
Strategy 4-Identify and Address Challenges			
Chapter 12-Challenges			
41: Analyze Your Workplace Opportunities and Threats			
42: Identify Sources for Your 360 Degree Feedback			
43: Identify Your Personal Board of Directors			
44: Connect Challenges to Job Responsibilities			
Strategy 5-Implement Success Methods			
Chapter 13-Complete the Strategies Grid			
45: Summarize the Research			
46: Connect Success Methods to Trends			
47: Connect Success Methods to Job Responsibilities			
48: Complete Your Strategies Grid			

you. It should fit within the timeframe you have between developing your own plan and your next performance review. The Action Boxes in this chapter provide a structure from which you can continue to build your performance review Strategies Grid and a more comprehensive Action Plan for *Exceeding Expectations.*

After many years of setting priorities, Sally found the best way to reach achievable goals is her 1-2-3 system. She lists her priorities in no particular order, then rates them as: 1-Very important, 2-Sort of important, 3-Not important. Sally takes all the 'Very important' items and rates them again as: 1-Must have, 2-Would be nice to have, 3-Can live without it. Then Sally breaks them down one last time, taking the 'Must have' items and listing them as either: 1-Must have now, 2-Must have soon, or 3-Must have but willing to wait.

Sally has become much more confident in her ability to set priorities that are important to her. She now moves forward, even if in baby steps; and accomplishes those things that are most important to her.

**Develop a system that allows you to prioritize
what is most important to you.**

In addition to the priorities you noted in Action Box 49, throughout the book you have committed to actions that you will take as you advance your performance review strategies. You identified dates by which you would complete the exercises, and/ or time intervals for reviewing or updating them. Action Plans help keep you moving forward. Summarize them in **Action Box 50**.

In Action Box 48, you completed your Strategies Grid. Earlier in the book you defined with whom you need to strategically communicate this information. You've also defined the message you need to communicate to these people or the information you need

ACTION BOX 50: Complete Step 2 of Your Performance Review Action Plan

Action Box	Commitments
1: Write Your Strategic Communications Goal	
34: Plan Your Accomplishments Reservoir(s)	
35: Plan Your Kind Words and Compliments Bin(s)	
36: Make Your CV Action Plan	
37: Make Your Resume Action Plan	
48: Complete Your Strategies Grid	

to seek from others. Use **Action Box 51** to capture this information. Referring back to Action Boxes 5 (Your Manager's Influencers), 42 (360 Degree Feedback) and 43 (Personal Board of Directors) for the people you need to reach, as well as Action Boxes 38 (Personal Brand) and 39 (Visible Value) regarding your strategic messages. Since your manager should be at the top of your target list, we've included that person as the first one on your list.

I, Tricia, have identified my manager's influencers and reach out regularly to my own personal board of directors to stay connected to what is happening within my work environment. In my most recent action planning process, I identified the information I needed to share within these groups to remain visible in my changing organization. My communication target includes the leaders within my organization and my peers who lead similar programs.

ACTION BOX 51: Complete Step 3 of Your Performance Review Action Plan

Compile the Action Plan components for your strategic communications.

Target	Message
Your Manager	Example: Accomplished 35% growth in Widget 432 sales

What additional actions will you take regarding your strategic communications?

Example: Begin monthly update report distributed to manager and peers

My communication message includes how I create collaborative partnerships, lead inside and outside the organization, and bring visibility and value to the organization. According to my plan, I share this message at the conclusion of each major initiative or event hosted by my program. This ensures my message is shared throughout the year and not just at performance review time.

Manageable Steps

Establishing manageable action steps toward your goals will help yield success. You have defined actions and steps throughout this book to move you forward in your career and to advance you toward *Exceeding Expectations*.

You have noted your high priorities, but sometimes it is difficult to take the first step toward achieving the goal. Action planning includes breaking down the tasks into actionable, doable short-term goals that move you toward completion of an exercise or reaching your goal.

Action Planning Next Steps

Priority Action	Next Steps
Create a Kind Words and Compliments Bin	1. Create a file for all your kind words and compliments 2. Go through your files, pulling out all the kind words and compliments 3. Put all kind words and compliments in the created file
Develop Strategies Grid Strategy 1: Job Responsibilities	1. Find current job description 2. Brainstorm all current job responsibilities 3. Find or define your organization's mission/vision/goals 4. Rewrite current job responsibilities as strategic job responsibilities

Use **Action Box 52** to identify your top two priorities and the next actions required to make progress on these priorities.

Have you committed to too much? I, Danielle, often find myself getting excited about what I can accomplish and over-committing. Review what you've written in Action Box 52 and make sure your prioritized Action Plan can be accomplished. Committing to a small task you can complete by your deadline is much better than committing to a large task that becomes a daunting "to do."

ACTION BOX 52: Identify Priorities of Your Performance Review Action Plan

My number one priority is _____ .

I will complete this by _____ (insert target date).

Steps I need to take to complete this include: _____

_____

_____

_____

I will *(insert specific first step you need to take)*_____

_____

_____

by _____ (insert date).

. . . .

My number two priority is _____ .

I will complete this by _____ (insert target date).

Steps I need to take to complete this include: _____

_____

_____

_____

I will *(insert specific first step you need to take)*_____

_____

_____

by _____ (insert date).

Kale attended a workshop where the instructor had suggested developing a Curriculum Vitae (CV) as a means of tracking his accomplishments and job experiences. It seemed overwhelming to compile all that he needed to create his CV. Kale had been working for the same company for nearly 10 years and had barely kept his resume updated. He certainly did not have a running list of all his accomplishments, but he did have records in various places and copies of past performance reviews and goal reports.

Kale had no idea where to start. He finally decided the CV was a priority when he was asked to apply for an industry award. Kale focused on one section of the CV at a time. It took a while to finish, but by taking one section at a time and working on it at a manageable pace, he was able to get it done. And he was honored with an award!

Creating manageable steps turns a daunting task into a doable task.

Implementation Strategy

Implementing your Action Plan requires a strategy. Evaluate the Performance Review Action Plan you have defined in Action Boxes 49 through 52 (Performance Review Action Steps 1-3) and set additional deadlines or milestones for yourself. Create a strategy that will keep you focused on your performance review process throughout the year. Plan at least one activity per month that requires you to give yourself a little time to prepare for your future, career and success.

I, Tricia, know keeping records of my accomplishments is important for my performance review. I block off time in my calendar each month to update my resume and CV. I may not need to spend much time on this effort each month; but by putting it on my calendar, I remember to focus monthly on my performance review strategy. If my resume or CV is updated, I can take the

Sydney was preparing for a career development meeting with her manager and felt lost. A friend suggested that she create an Action Plan, but this was a bit overwhelming for Sydney. She had several tasks that needed completing and didn't quite know where to start. After considering the highest priority items – the tasks that were critical to have completed for the meeting – Sydney was able to move into action.

She identified the most critical piece, broke that task into smaller actions and began moving forward one small step at a time. Once that was completed, she moved on to the next task. Sydney didn't complete all the tasks she wanted to before the meeting but, by prioritizing, she was able to complete the most important ones and have a successful meeting with her manager.

Set priorities and take your Action Plan one step at a time.

time to review goals, project requirements and strategic processes. I ensure that I keep moving toward my definition of success.

Take time to reflect on where you are and where you are headed. You have set your top two priorities in Action Box 52 and defined some of the next steps required. Use **Action Box 53** to identify the activities you will commit to for each of the next 12 months.

It may take you all year to address your top two priorities or you may have additional Action Plan priorities you'd like to address this year. Perhaps you plan to focus on defining job responsibilities this month, updating your resume next month and continuing through the rest of your Action Plan in following months. You should take time throughout the year to review the exercises you have completed throughout this book and revise them as your situation changes. Decide what your strategy is to implement your Action Plan and make some monthly commitments to move you toward performance review success.

ACTION BOX 53: Make Monthly Commitments

Month	Commitment
Example: January	*Example: Distribute monthly update report; Begin accomplishments reservoir; Review and update five-year goals*

Implementation strategies can take many forms and you must decide what works best for you. You may need several strategies and they may change over time as your situation changes. Some successful implementation strategies we have used include the following:

- Incorporate your Action Plan into your daily tasks and work flow(s)

- Share your Action Plan and strategies with your manager(s) and your personal board of directors, ask them to hold you to it, and make it a part of your meeting discussions

- Take one step at a time as you work through your priorities

- Post your Action Plan or your year-one or intermediate goals in a place where you will see it throughout the day as a reminder of your priorities and focus

- Reserve time on your calendar once a month to reevaluate your Performance Review Action Plan and the Action Boxes and Strategies in this book

- Create a Career Action Plan Group that operates like a weight-loss competition or book club, and hold each other accountable for monthly goals

- Develop a reward system for yourself for accomplishing each step on your Action Plan; celebrate those accomplishments!

Immediate Next Actions

You now have priorities and a view of what you would like to accomplish in the next year. Take the number one priority you identified in Action Box 52 (Performance Review Action Plan Priorities) and consider what you can do today. What can you do **now** to take that first step in your Action Plan? By considering what you can truly accomplish today, this week and this month, you can begin to make progress in manageable action steps.

Block off 30 minutes of time tomorrow so you can consider what your next step may be or locate last year's performance review or this year's review forms. Whatever your first step is, identify it. Taking one small step that is independent of all other actions can get you moving on your top priority. Often that is all we need, that first step, to get us moving. Use **Action Box 54** to define your first steps.

ACTION BOX 54: Identify Immediate Next Actions

Today I will: _____

_____

_____

_____

This week I will: _____

_____

_____

_____

_____

This month I will: _____

_____

_____

_____

_____

Completing all the exercises in this book and creating your Performance Review Action Plan is just a beginning. To *Exceed Expectations* and to advance toward your goals, you must continually revisit, revise and reconsider what you have done and where you are going. You must keep your performance review and career development strategy in perpetual action. Manage your Performance Review Action Plan and continue to take the steps necessary to advance toward your goals. Action Plans are dynamic documents that need to be reviewed and revised on a regular basis.

Perpetual Motion Isn't Enough

Just keeping your Action Plan moving isn't enough. Movement is good, but if your movement is in a direction counter to your goals or in conflict with your manager or organization, you will have challenges *Exceeding Expectations* on your performance review. As you work through your Performance Review Action Plan, new information and new circumstances may arise requiring a change of plans. If you do not adjust along the way, you can lose sight of the environment in which you work and make it difficult to excel in your performance review. Staying the course, regardless of the situation, is dangerous.

When your performance review is over, your Performance Review Action Plan has not ended. Start thinking about next year. Set your goals for your next review. Clarify your job description and update any changes. Clearly define the metrics you will be judged on. This is a continual process.

We are all constantly shaped and reshaped by life and career experiences, the people we meet, our feelings, our environment and our changing perceptions. Give yourself a day every year to revisit and rework the Action Boxes and Strategies. Make sure

Amanda's career and personal life were on track and headed exactly where she always thought she wanted to go. She had a challenging job with lots of travel and responsibility. She had been married for 10 years and had two wonderful children.

Amanda was offered an international position and her family decided it was a great opportunity for them all. The career shift allowed her to experience a different work environment and a different pace of life. Her eyes were opened to dream job characteristics she had never considered before.

Amanda was truly astonished at how much her dream job shifted as a result of that experience. Experiencing a culture that put less emphasis on the number of hours worked and more emphasis on a balanced perspective changed her aspirations. Amanda's career has continued to prosper, but she now values a position that allows her to work remotely part of the time and travel less.

Your career plan will shift to reflect changes in your experiences and motivations.

you are on the path that is important **today** rather than what was important last year.

This is something I, Danielle, have been doing for years. Now I look forward to my quiet day of reflection about myself. I have kept every year's information in the same notebook and I enjoy looking back and seeing how much I have changed.

We have seen the Strategies Grid and the Balanced Performance Review Model work. We have experienced it ourselves, time and time again, throughout our careers. When we fully embrace the model and implement our own strategy and personal Performance Review Action Plan, we *Exceed Expectations* on our performance reviews. When we skip steps, forget to align our goals and job responsibilities to the organization, or lessen our communications

Estela graduated from college and began teaching at an inner-city school. In the beginning, she loved her job, especially the summers off. The job wore on her quickly though, and she determined that it must be the inner-city aspects, so she moved to a suburban school. It was worse!

Estela was so confused because she was doing what she always wanted to do, was very involved in the extracurricular activities at the school, and was in "the perfect job for her personality." What was wrong? Estela enrolled in a workshop to help her understand herself better. As she began to work through the various exercises and create a career plan, she realized that teaching is the perfect job for her; however, she needed to teach adults rather than children. She made a shift to corporate training and now loves her job.

Staying the course doesn't always work. Revisit the Action Boxes annually to discover the right path for you today.

to our manager or other key stakeholders, our reviews are less than satisfactory.

You have done it! You have the tools and the information you need to strategically communicate your job performance successes and to *Exceed Expectations* in your performance review. You have explored your visible value and priorities, defined your goals and created an Action Plan to move you strategically forward. You have the strategy to *Exceed Expectations* and to take control of your performance review, the performance review process and your career. Put your strategy into perpetual action with manageable steps and you will be successful.

The Strategies are straightforward:
   Strategy 1: Understand Job Responsibilities
   Strategy 2: Define Goals or Objectives
   Strategy 3: Collect and Communicate Accomplishments

Strategy 4: Identify and Address Challenges
Strategy 5: Implement Success Methods

The Strategies Grid puts it all together and your Performance Review Action Plan puts your strategies into motion.

Strategies Grid

Strategy 1	Strategy 2	Strategy 3	Strategy 4	Strategy 5
Job Responsibilities	Goals or Objectives	Accomplishments	Challenges	Success Methods
1.				
2.				
3.				

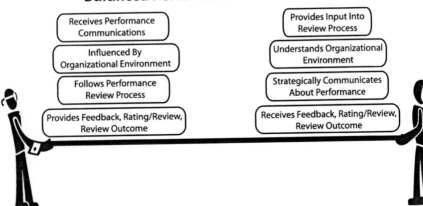

Balanced Performance Review Model

James had worked as an IT contract employee for a large oil firm for many years. After accepting a permanent position with the company, James decided he needed to brush up on his performance review skills. It had been many years since he had worked for anyone other than himself. In addition, James' manager doesn't really know what he does on a daily basis – only what the outcome of his work should look like.

So, James attended the 825 Basics™ course, *Don't Hit the Snooze: Managing Your Performance Review*. The week after the class, he had his performance review. James used all of the tips he learned in class and his review went very well. James just took over the performance review, and his manager, who didn't really know what he does, really appreciated it. James was rated as a high performer and received a good bonus and raise as well. He *Exceeded Expectations!*

Take the initiative in your performance review. Take control and you will *Exceed Expectations!*

Chapter 14 Takeaways

Implement Your Strategy

- To prepare for your performance review meeting, follow four steps:

    1. Complete the Strategies Grid

    2. Complete your organization's performance review forms

    3. Provide information to your manager in advance

    4. Have a plan for the performance review meeting

- Develop a system that allows you to prioritize what is most important to you.

- Set priorities and take your Action Plan one step at a time.

- Creating manageable steps turns a daunting task into a doable task.

- Your career plan will shift to reflect changes in your experiences and motivations.

- Staying the course doesn't always work. Revisit the Action Boxes annually to discover the right path for you.

- Take the initiative in your performance review. Take control and you will *Exceed Expectations*!

Our hope is that you now know what needs to be done. You have the tools to put your Action Plan in place. Embrace the Balanced Performance Review Model and *Exceed Expectations* on your next performance review.

We helped you shift the power and total responsibility from your manager to both of you. You **can** aim for a different vision of success. You **can** aim for your definition of success. You **can** drive the process so that your goals have a better chance of being met before, during and after the performance review.

You **can** *Exceed Expectations!*

Additional Resources

Table of Action Boxes

Chapter 1	**The Balanced Model**	**1**
ACTION BOX 1:	Write Your Strategic Communications Goal	9
Chapter 3	**Understand the Performance Review Process**	**23**
ACTION BOX 2:	Assess Past Performance Reviews	25
ACTION BOX 3:	Explore Your Performance Review Process	27-34
ACTION BOX 4:	Identify Your Manager's Performance Review Style	37
ACTION BOX 5:	Describe Your Manager's Influencers	41
ACTION BOX 6:	Identify Valued Peer Skills	44
ACTION BOX 7:	Describe Your Organization's Rating Structure	46
Chapter 4	**Explore Workplace Priorities**	**49**
ACTION BOX 8:	Recognize Your Workplace Priorities	51
ACTION BOX 9:	Note Your Manager's Priorities	55
ACTION BOX 10:	Describe Your Organization's Priorities	57
ACTION BOX 11:	Compare Priorities	58
Chapter 5	**Explore External Performance Review Influences**	**67**
ACTION BOX 12:	Examine Your External Network	68
ACTION BOX 13:	Identify External Network Needs	75
Chapter 6	**Define Performance Review Success**	**77**
ACTION BOX 14:	Describe Your Idea of Performance Review Success	80
ACTION BOX 15:	Define Your Manager's Performance Review Success	82
ACTION BOX 16:	Define Your Organization's Performance Review Success	89
Strategy 1	Understand Job Responsibilities	91
Chapter 7	Define Your Job	93
ACTION BOX 17:	List Your Official Job Responsibilities	95
ACTION BOX 18:	Write Your Current Job Responsibilities	96
ACTION BOX 19:	Define Your Organization's Goals and/or Mission	98
ACTION BOX 20:	Rewrite to Identify Strategic Job Responsibilities	100
Strategy 2	**Define Goals or Objectives**	**103**

Chapter 8	**Reveal the Real You**	**105**
ACTION BOX 21:	List Your Likes and Dislikes	110
ACTION BOX 22:	Identify Your Strengths	112
ACTION BOX 23:	Align Your Strengths Strategically	113
ACTION BOX 24:	List Compliments	115
ACTION BOX 25:	List Your Weaknesses	117
ACTION BOX 26:	Address Your Weaknesses	120
ACTION BOX 27:	Record Comments	121
Chapter 9	**Define Your Goals**	**127**
ACTION BOX 28:	Identify Your Dream Job	130-134
ACTION BOX 29:	Define Your Lifetime Goals	139
ACTION BOX 30:	Define Your Five-Year Goals	141
ACTION BOX 31:	Define Your One-Year Goals	144
ACTION BOX 32:	Connect Personal Goals to Job Responsibilities	148
ACTION BOX 33:	Connect Job Specific Goals to Job Responsibilities	151
Strategy 3	**Collect and Communicate Accomplishments**	**153**
Chapter 10	**Collect Your Accomplishments**	**155**
ACTION BOX 34:	Plan Your Accomplishments Reservoir(s)	160
ACTION BOX 35:	Plan Your Kind Words and Compliments Bin(s)	162
ACTION BOX 36:	Make Your CV Action Plan	165
ACTION BOX 37:	Make Your Resume Action Plan	167
Chapter 11	**Communicate Your Accomplishments**	**169**
ACTION BOX 38:	Plan Your Personal Brand	174
ACTION BOX 39:	Make Your Visible Value Shine	182
ACTION BOX 40:	Connect Accomplishments to Job Responsibilities	190
Strategy 4	**Identify and Address Challenges**	**193**
Chapter 12	**Challenges**	**195**
ACTION BOX 41:	Analyze Your Workplace Opportunities and Threats	197
ACTION BOX 42:	Identify Sources for Your 360 Degree Feedback	201
ACTION BOX 43:	Identify Your Personal Board of Directors	204
ACTION BOX 44:	Connect Challenges to Job Responsibilities	206
Strategy 5	**Implement Success Methods**	**209**
Chapter 13	**Complete the Strategies Grid**	**211**
ACTION BOX 45:	Summarize Your Research	213-214
ACTION BOX 46:	Connect Success Methods to Trends	216
ACTION BOX 47:	Connect Success Methods to Job Responsibilities	218
ACTION BOX 48:	Complete Your Strategies Grid	220

Chapter 14   Implement Your Strategy   223
  ACTION BOX 49: Complete Step 1 of Your Performance Review Action Plan   226-228
  ACTION BOX 50: Complete Step 2 of Your Performance Review Action Plan   230
  ACTION BOX 51: Complete Step 3 of Your Performance Review Action Plan   231
  ACTION BOX 52: Identify Priorities of Your Performance Review Action Plan 233
  ACTION BOX 53: Make Monthly Commitments   236
  ACTION BOX 54: Identify Immediate Next Actions   238

Words to Spark Thoughts

Sometimes you just need the right word or phrase to get your creative juices flowing. Here is a list of words and phrases that may help provide you the strategic action word for your job description, the perfect descriptor for your amazing performance, or the right phrase to showcase your accomplishments. To find more words, perform an Internet search for "descriptive words" or "action verbs" or look for key words for resumes.

Descriptors

Accurate
Action Oriented
Adaptable
Analytical
Artistic
Attentive
Authoritative
Autonomous
Big Picture Thinker
Business Minded
Caring
Charismatic
Common Sense
Competent
Competitive
Conceptual
Confident

Conservative
Consultant
Creative
Decisive
Dedicated
Dependable
Detail Oriented
Diplomatic
Direct
Disciplined
Driven
Efficient
Empathetic
Energetic
Enthusiastic
Ethical
Exciting
Expert

Fair
Fast Paced
Flexible
Friendly
Funny
Handles Pressure
Hands On
Hard Worker
Harmonious
Helpful
Honest
Humorous
Ideal
Independent
Innovative
Integrity
Intelligent
Intuitive

Knowledgeable
Leader
Learns Quickly
Listener
Logical
Loyal
Mature
Memorable
Modern
Money Minded
Motivated
Objective
Optimistic
Orderly
Outdoors
Overbooked
Patient
Persistent
Pioneer
Poised
Practical
Pragmatic
Prestigious
Proactive
Professional
Pulled Together
Qualified
Quality
Quick
Realistic
Reliable
Responsible
Risk Taker
Routine

Self Motivated
Self Reliant
Self Respect
Sensitive
Sharp
Sincere
Smart
Spiritual
Spontaneous
Stable
Thorough
Thoughtful
Visible
Visual
Well Rounded
Willing
Witty

Actions
Achieve
Administer
Advance
Advise
Analyze
Appraise
Arbitrate
Arrange
Assemble
Assign
Audit
Balance
Belong
Budget
Develop

Calculate
Challenge
Change
Clarify
Classic
Coach
Collect
Communicate
Compensation
Complete
Compute
Conduct
Consolidate
Contract
Control
Coordinate
Cooperate
Create
Critique
Cultivate
Define
Delegate
Demonstrate
Design
Develop
Devise
Diagnose
Edit
Enable
Encourage
Endure
Enlighten
Enlist
Establish

Evaluate

Examine

Execute

Experience

Explain

Extrapolate

Facilitate

Fashion

Fire

Forecast

Formulate

Gather

Generate

Govern

Grow

Guide

Hire

Identify

Implement

Improve

Increase

Influence

Inform

Initiate

Inspect

Install

Interpret

Interview

Invent

Invest

Investigate

Limit

Maintain

Manage

Manipulate

Mediate

Merge

Moderate

Negotiate

Network

Obtain

Operate

Organize

Perceive

Perform

Persevere

Persuade

Plan

Play

Power

Present

Prioritize

Process

Produce

Program

Propose

Publically Speak

Reason

Recommend

Recognize

Reconcile

Recruit

Redesign

Reduce

Refer

Render

Research

Result

Review

Revise

Schedule

Secure

Sell

Service

Set Up

Shape

Share

Simplify

Solve

Speak

Staff

Start

Streamline

Stimulate

Structure

Supervise

Systems

Teamwork

Time Management

Track

Trade

Train

Translate

Transform

Troubleshoot

Trust

Understand

Unify

Validate

Value

Verify

About the Authors

*E*xceeds Expectations is the culmination of years of personal experiences and the development of workshops and trainings to help professionals successfully navigate the workplace. Tricia Berry and Danielle Forget Shield have supported each other and mentored countless others for over 15 years. Through 825 Basics, LLC, a career enhancement training company that has a proven track record of inspiring professionals to create plans for success, they apply problem solving techniques to the workplace. The performance review process described in *Exceeds Expectations* demonstrates their action oriented style that yields immediate results.

Tricia Berry, MBA

It is important to Tricia Berry, MBA that every professional has a career plan and an understanding of themselves and their environment. She is an engaging and inspiring speaker whose workshops and presentations coach people how to create a plan for their future. Tricia is the Executive Vice President and Chief Creative Officer for 825 Basics, LLC.

Tricia has over 15 years experience in training, presentations, workshop development, coaching and process management. Tricia's varied experiences include career training, large volunteer program management, professional speaking, and workshop and training development and implementation. Tricia received her BS Chemical Engineering degree from The University of Texas at Austin and her MBA from the University of Houston—Clear Lake.

Tricia is currently the Director of the Women in Engineering Program at The University of Texas at Austin where she is responsible for leading the efforts on recruitment and retention of women in the Cockrell School of Engineering. Concurrently, she directs the Texas Girls Collaborative Project and serves as a program assessment consultant. Prior career experiences include positions in engineering design and research at The Dow Chemical Company. Tricia resides in Austin, TX with her husband, James Farone, and their two sons.

Danielle Forget Shield, PE, MBA

For over 10 years Danielle Forget Shield, PE, MBA has been providing entertaining and useful presentations that harness the power of interactive discussions with audience members. She is the President and Chief Executive Officer of 825 Basics, LLC

Danielle has extensive experience in public speaking, workshop development, career coaching and organizational management. Her excitement comes from experience in implementing the methods she teaches and seeing those she has mentored successfully navigate their careers. Danielle received her BS in Civil Engineering from Washington University in St. Louis and her MBA from the University of St. Thomas in Houston.

Danielle's corporate experience includes positions as Vice President for Sindicatum Carbon Capital, an alternative energy company, and Director of Engineering & Environmental Compliance for WCA Waste Corporation. Previous careers experiences with WCA, Drake Beam Morin, Waste Management and BFI/Allied Waste included positions in sales, training, consulting, engineering and operations management. Danielle resides in Houston, TX with her husband, Chris Shield, and their three children.

CPSIA information can be obtained at www.ICGtesting.com
Printed in the USA
LVOW011850141011

250591LV00002B/2/P

3 1524 00577 0302